U.S. LATINO LITERATURE:

AN ESSAY AND ANNOTATED BIBLIOGRAPHY

MARC ZIMMERMAN

MARCH/ABRAZO PRESS

Library of Congress Cataloging-in-Publication Data
Zimmerman, Marc

Main entry under title: *U.S. Latino Literature: An Essay and Annotated Bibliography.*

1. U.S. Hispanic Literature.   2. Chicano Literature.
3. Puerto Rican Literature.   4. Cuban Literature.
5. Reference   I. Zimmerman, Marc.

This is the revised, expanded and corrected second edition of *U.S. Latino Literature: The Creative Expression of a People*, commissioned and published by the Chicago Public Library in 1990, as part of the Library's project, "Serving the Hispanic User: Promoting Latino Literature," made possible by a federal Library Services and Construction Act grant awarded by the Illinois State Library and proposed and coordinated by Mary Ellen Quinn.

This edition was commissioned by a **Director's Discretionary Grant from the Illinois Humanities Council**, with support from the **National Endowment of the Humanities**. The intention is to update and highlight the growing Chicago and Illinois contribution to a burgeoning literary corpus.

Copyright (C) 1992 Marc Zimmerman.
ISBN 1-877636-01-0

Cover Design: Cynthia Gallaher
Cover Drawing: Carlos A. Cortez

El Movimiento Artístico Chicano
MARCH, Inc.
MARCH/ Abrazo Press
P.O. Box 2890
Chicago, IL 60690

Printed in the United States of America

Dedicated to the memory of
Sammy Medina Soler
(1963-1991),
querido hijo de Esther
y hermano de sus hermanas.
Boricua,
todavía aquí en este libro
y en nuestros corazones.

TABLE OF CONTENTS

PREFACE   *3*

U.S. LATINOS: THEIR CULTURE AND LITERATURE   9

I. LATINO LITERATURE IN THE CULTURAL PROCESS   9
II.   LATINOS AND THEIR CULTURE   11
A. Identity   11
B. Some Definitions   12
C. Some Questions about the Future of Latinos   16

III. U.S. LATINO LITERATURE:
HISTORY AND DEVELOPMENT   18
A. Latino Populations and Three Phases
of Migration Literature   18
B. The Development of Chicano Literature   21
C. Puerto Rican Literature in the U.S.   28
D. Cuban and Other U.S. Latino Literatures   36

IV. POSTMODERN PERSPECTIVES
AND FINAL THOUGHTS   40
A. Some Key Perspectives   40
B. Postmodern Multicultural Crossovers   42
C. Literature, the Midwest and Future Developments   44

**LATINO LITERATURE: A SELECTED
AND ANNOTATED BIBLIOGRAPHY**   *49*

I. GENERAL LATINO ANTHOLOGIES   49

II. CHICANO LITERATURE   54
A. Anthologies of Chicano Literature   54
    1. General Chicano Literature Anthologies   54
    2. Chicano Oral and Folk Traditions   56
    3. Chicano Poetry Anthologies   58
    4. Chicano Short Fiction Anthologies   59
    5. Chicano Drama Anthologies   60

B. Works by Individual Chicano Writers   61
    1. Chicano Poetry   61

2.	Chicano Novel and Long (Non-Personal) Narrative	76
3.	Chicano Autobiography	95
4.	Chicano Short Fiction, Essays, etc.	98
5.	Chicano Drama	107

III. U.S. PUERTO RICAN LITERATURE 110
A. Anthologies of U.S. Puerto Rican Literature 110
B. Works by Individual U.S. Puerto Rican Writers 112
   1. U.S. Puerto Rican Poetry 112
   2. U.S. Puerto Rican Personal Narrative and Novel 118
   3. U.S. Puerto Rican Short Fiction and Essays 123
   4. U.S. Puerto Rican Drama 126
   5. Translated Island-Based Puerto Rican Literature on the U.S. Immigration Experience 127
   6. Untranslated Island-Based Puerto Rican Literature on the U.S. Immigration Experience 128

IV. U.S. CUBAN LITERATURE 130
A. Anthologies of U.S. Cuban Literature 130
B. Works by Individual U.S. Cuban Writers 131
   1. U.S. Cuban Poetry 131
   2. U.S. Cuban Fiction 132
   3. U.S. Cuban Drama 136

V. LATINO-TENDING U.S. LATIN AMERICAN WRITING 137

VI. LATINO CHILDREN AND YOUNG ADULT BOOKS 139

VII. CHICANESQUE LITERATURE 140

VIII. SECONDARY MATERIALS 141
A. Books on Latino Literature (General) 141
B. Books on Chicano Literature 143
   1. Recent Bibliographies 143
   2. Criticism 144
C. Books on U.S. Puerto Rican Literature 154
D. Books on U.S. Cuban Literature 155

PREFACE

Since the manuscript for the first edition of this text was completed, countless new works of and about U.S. Latino literature have appeared. The list of recent publications is a remarkable one, including major novels and poetry collections, as well as pathbreaking theoretically-driven critical texts, as integral to a spurt of cultural production that raises fundamental questions about the overall field and its conceptualization. Among the new theory-oriented works are Juan Bruce-Novoa's *RetroSpace*, Ramón Saldívar's *Chicano Narrative*, Juan Flores's *Divided Borders*, and the state-of-the-art collection, Héctor Calderón and José David Saldívar's *Criticism in the Borderlands.* In addition, a first "cultural studies"-oriented collection, Angie Chabram and Rosalinda Fregoso's *Chicana/o Cultural Representations: Reframing Critical Discourses*, has appeared; and so has new, feminist crossover text of theory and creativity, *The Sexuality of Latinas*, (see Part VIII the Annotations for details on these books). Even putting aside the latter collection, it should be noted that all the new works mentioned here are significantly inflected by feminist theory; furthermore, sufficient selections from theoretical works in progress, as well as a number of significant feminist creative works, have appeared to point toward the weighty contribution of Latina feminism to reconstructing Latino literary theory. And, it should be noted as well, that many creative works by midwest and specifically Chicago-origin or residence writers have appeared in this brief period to contribute to our reconceptualizing efforts.

In addition to this internal configuration, a whole range of polemics have come center stage--debates over U.S. and Latin American literary canons (as well as their possible inter-relatedness under the rubric of "New World Writing," etc.); over "political correctness" and "multi-culturalism" or "multicultural literacy"; over possibilities of "literary difference," "resistance" and "subaltern voice"; over the "transformative difference within difference" constituted by feminist and homosexual texts. These controversial questions, in the midst of the overall effort of mapping contemporary, postmodern culture, have brought at least certain works and indeed the entire field of U.S. Latino literature to a level of recognized significance that they had never before achieved.

To be sure, Chicano literature, as a large, creatively developing ensemble, has dominated the Latino critical debate and threatened to colonize and distort perspectives with respect to not only non-Chicano Latino texts but even Chicano or *mexicano* ones that, for regional or other reasons, do not quite fit the Southwest-centered models. Flores's book, and also Elías Miguel Muñoz's *Desde ésta orilla*, enable us to project points of Puerto Rican and Cuban similarity and difference. The appearance of exploratory fiction works by Chicanas like Ana Castillo and Sandra Cisneros, along with the first U.S. Puerto Rican women's novels other than those by Nicholasa Mohr (by Carmen de Monteflores, Judith Ortiz Cofer and Carole Fernández), as well as the appearance also of the first major Latina works of fiction by a Cuban, Cristina García and (the most remarkable breakthrough) a Dominican, Julia Alvarez, provide bases for projecting a broader view of the Latino field. And what might *The Mambo Kings*, or recent texts by John Rechy and Isabel Allende tell us about overall Latina/o questions?

There may well be at least a problematic distortion in using such terms as "Chicano" or "Latino"--which may designate not a "people," as the romantic subtitle of this book's first edition suggests, but, rather, very diverse groups with such regionally inflected origins and situations, such class, generational and contextual differentiations, etc., that the unifying designation may seem more a creation of a non-Latino professor or a hoped for, rather than necessarily existent, response to Anglo hegemony.

This new edition at least partially reflects the advanced state of Chicano literature and Latino literature as a whole in their interconnection with contemporary theory. The revised introduction to our text attempts to address some of the questions mentioned above, including those relating to Latino cultural identity as the context for the literary works; it also touches on the way in which the recent theoretical and creative works change our way of conceiving the literary corpus, and how that corpus has been extended by new feminist, new non-Chicano/Puerto Rican/Cuban works; the introduction hints at how the growing Chicago and other midwestern contributions seem to point toward further reconceptualizations of the field. This is not to claim that the revised essay is now the "last word" on its subject. Rather, the new perspectives are only lightly registered, while the annotations themselves involve descriptions of works and theorizations which require elucidation beyond what time and circumstances permitted here.

As the book appears, perhaps Norma Alarcón, Angie Chabram, Rosaura Sánchez, Sonia Saldívar-Hull or other leading Chicana feminist critics will publish their long-awaited volumes that will further transform the field. Perhaps Juan Flores's contribution will create a context for a Puerto Rican feminist breakthrough; and perhaps Ellen McCracken, Eliana Rivero or other critics will write trans-Latina studies that will make this present book even more inadequate than it presently is. And of course we may expect creative experimentation to go beyond theory and demand its further reformulation.

All of these caveats stated, I still maintain that the introduction and the book as a whole will be valuable for many readers wishing some initial orientation to this fascinating and expanding field. I only hope that readers will find this text of use and that it will stir many to explore at least some of the works described.

The bibliography itself was specifically designed for new readers of Latino literature. It is not complete, nor is meant to be; but I have tried to include most of the major works, or at least one or more representative works, by each of the more important or successful writers. Other than representativity, my criteria in selection have been based on overlapping and sometimes contradictory considerations of language, subject matter and orientation. Thus, I have distinguished between Mexican texts on Chicano life, immigration, etc., and Chicano texts dealing with Mexican life, excluding the former and including the latter. In like manner (though the problem is more difficult and I have sometimes been inconsistent), I have chosen Nuyoricans writing about San Juan over island writers writing about New York. In some cases, such as René Marqués's *La Carreta (The Oxcart)*, I have violated my own criteria because of the great importance of the work in question for immigration literature, and also because the work, deeply ingrained in indigenous Puerto Rican discourse, has been translated. On the other hand, with a parallel case in Mexican literature, *Los Desarraigados*, a play dealing very negatively with Chicanos, seen as uprooted Mexicans, or *pochos*, I have excluded the work, because it seems to have had little impact on Chicano literature and it has not been translated.

Clearly preference has been given to English-language texts or Spanish texts that have been translated. But questions of Spanish or English are not so important as the kinds of Spanish and English. An educated Puerto Rican may write a standard English in translation, but it is not necessarily a New York-acculturated discourse. Even if the

English conforms to New York norms, the Spanish may not do so. As in language, so in subject matter or orientation to it (from an island point of view, almost everything in New York is negative). My *inclination* (though not law) has been to chose the U.S.-tending works--the ones that may represent U.S. ethnic literature, even if ultimately they represent a veering from ethnicity back to older roots or toward total mainstreaming and assimilation. On this basis, I have excluded many works by Puerto Rican university professors living in the U.S., to the degree that they have quite successfully maintained their relation to the island's and thereby more broadly Caribbean and Latin American literary production (cf. the discussion in my introduction below). On the other hand, I have included professor-writer Luz Umpierre, while I have excluded a fine writer like Rosario Ferré. Perhaps Bruce-Novoa's pressure to extend the literary paradigm and a local pressure to include Chicago writers have led me to include works by Sheila Ortiz Taylor, Cecile Piñeda and Laurence Gonzales. But there are other mainstream-tending works that I perhaps should have included, but could not finally get myself to include, even though I might have suspected them of being more subtly "ethnic" than others that did make the list.

This question of criteria involves almost insoluble complexities; and they pertain perhaps most significantly to Cuban and other non-Mexican and non-Puerto Rican writers as they emerge in the U.S. My rule with the Cubans was to include mainly those U.S.-based writers focused more on the immigrant experience than on questions of Cuban history, Fidel Castro and the like. On the one hand, I certainly felt an obligation to include several entries of an abundant and growing literature. But, on the other hand, the force of U.S. Cuban preoccupations with the island and middle class pursuits might have led to excluding many writers and works. My unhappy compromise was to focus on those writers who were clearly part of a U.S./Cuban Continental world as opposed to a more strictly island one in style, language, subject matter or orientation.

The issue of criteria for volumes such as this will only become more complex as years go by, with increasing numbers of Latin Americans from various countries now living in the U.S., and with many more Chicano, Puerto Rican and Dominican writers with middle and upperclass backgrounds, as well as advanced literary educations. In this regard, this edition, like the first, still attempts to toe the line, and maintain a concern with ethnic minority and working class orientations--even though I make a kind of transitional concession in the section listed as Part V of the *Annotations*, perhaps in recognition of the quixotic nature of an effort to maintain an episteme at least inflected by a concern with class and class struggle.

In addition to my own opinions and perceptions, I have drawn on many sources for my listings and descriptions, having had recourse to most of the major books and articles written about Latino literature. The most important sources for my Chicano annotations were Roberto G. Trujillo and Andrés Rodríguez, *Literatura Chicana: Creative and Critical Writings through 1984* (Encino, CA: Floricanto Press, 1985); Carl R. Shirley and Paula W. Shirley, *Understanding Chicano Literature* (Columbia, South Carolina: U. of South Carolina Press, 1988); Virginia Ramos Foster, "Literature," in David William Foster, ed., *Sourcebook of Hispanic Culture in the United States* (Chicago: American Library Association, 1982, pp. 86-111); and several numbers of *Lector*, a publication dealing with "Mexican American" writers.

For Puerto Rican materials, the main sources drawn on are Edna Acosta-Belén, "The Literature of the Puerto Rican Migration in the United States," in *ADE Bulletin*, no. 91 (Winter, 1988), pp. 56-62; and David William Foster, ed. *U.S. Puerto Rican Literature A Bibliography of Secondary Sources* (Westport, CT: Greenwood, 1983). For additional Puerto Rican perspectives, as well as notes on U.S. Cuban literature, I drew on Naomi E. Lindstrom, "Cuban and Continental Puerto Rican Literature," in Foster, ed., *Sourcebook of Hispanic Culture*, pp. 221-45. I also availed myself of the catalogue descriptions of Arte Público Press (*APP*), Bilingual Review Press (*BRP*) and Waterfront Press for succinct summaries and blurbs based on critical reviews from a variety of sources. I had frequent recourse to the two leading Latino literary/cultural journals, *Américas Review* (formerly, *Revista Chicano-Riqueña*) and *The Bilingual Review*.

For this edition, Carlos Cumpián and Cynthia Gallaher of the MARCH Research Collective suggested books and helped draft some entries (indicated by *MRC*); also, in some instances I have included recent texts which I knew to be important but which I could not secure or examine by deadline time (indicated by *NR*, for *Not Reviewed*). In the last analysis, however, I am responsible for the selection, the ordering, the bibliographical data and comments.

I have generally chosen to list books in relation to their most recent and available edition, often indicating the year of original publication in the body of my note; and I have chosen to order the works by a given author chronologically rather than alphabetically so that the author's development might more readily emerge.

Thanks to Carlos Cumpián and MARCH for their overall support in seeing to the publication of the book. Thanks to Pilar Medina, José Garza and UIC Latin American Studies students Scott Curry, José Candelas and Francisco Arcaute for their research help. Thanks to Mario Widel and Patricio Navia for help with computer-related problems. Thanks to Ellen McCracken for her CARE package; thanks finally to Frank Pettis, Mary Ellen Quinn and Esther Soler for their support and vision.

Marc Zimmerman, Chicago
12/17/91

U.S. LATINOS: THEIR CULTURE AND LITERATURE

I. LATINO LITERATURE IN THE CULTURAL PROCESS

In the past several years, with the remarkable growth and diversification of the U.S. Latino population, we have witnessed the emergence of a literature expressing Latino traditions, conflicts, and transformations. Contrary to common understanding, literature by Hispanics or Latinos, mainly in Spanish, but sometimes in English as well, has existed in what is now the U.S. since the sixteenth century; and a distinctly ethnic Latino literature has been evolving for well over a hundred years. With the emergence of U.S. Chicano and Puerto Rican social movements in the 1960s, a number of young Chicano and Nuyorican writers also surfaced and synthesized the bases for new literatures which were consciously and specifically ethnic in character and function.

Characterized by nostalgia for a fading past, by a critique of racial oppression and negative acculturation experiences in the fields, in the city neighborhoods, the schools, factories and homes, by bilingualisms, schizophrenic goal conflicts and sex role confusions, by cultural tensions, affirmations and anger, and by calls for reform, rebellion, revolution or other forms of opposition, the emergent Latino literatures of the 1960s attempted to serve as laboratories for the expression and then reconstruction of transformed Latin American and U.S. Southwest Hispano-Indian peoples into "Mexican-Americans" or "Chicanos," into "Nuyoricans" or other Ricans, and ultimately, into the problematic and questionable but aggregate we know today as "Hispanics" or "Latinos."

Of course, few people knew of the literatures emerging among the *chicanos* and *boricuas*. Professional writers and critics (non-Latinos almost all) were slow to recognize and come to respect even their greatest early achievements. It was common for budding Latino writers in different parts of the U.S. to be unaware of the existence of other Latino writers; and even when burgeoning Chicano and Puerto Rican literary movements had emerged in relation to growing Latino national consciousness and action, few Latinos living in the U.S. were aware of the literatures. But what could one expect when millions of Latinos only had limited functional literacy in Spanish or English and when most Latinos were consigned to blue-collar or no-collar jobs, if they found work at all? It took the first relatively largescale wave of Latino students in U.S. universities, in the context of the overall civil rights movement and the emergence of an anti-establishment, anti-Vietnam War counter culture, to produce both the writers and readers of these new literatures.

Where were the Latino writers in the sixties? Some were in colleges and universities, studying and sometimes even teaching. But others were in the countryside, doing stoop labor. And still more were in the cities, in their enclaves and *barrios*, in all the real and metaphorical jails and refuges provided for those marginalized by harsh and inhospitable urban circumstances. Of course some of them who could free themselves and grow actually found a way through the maze of bilingualisms and biculturalisms to express themselves, and indeed forge a new written language; and some of these writers even found their way into the few magazines and journals that would publish their work--or into the new publications they or friends created which served as outlets they otherwise had great difficulty finding in the U.S., in their own region or in the cities and towns where they congregated.

While starting as a "marginal, subcultural enterprise" whose promotion and study was restricted to small publications and small ethnic studies programs, U.S. Latino literature has recently received increasing attention in relation to the efforts to redefine and articulate the U.S. and Latin American literary canons, to deal with demands for multi-cultural curriculum and to explore the possibilities of cultural and symbolic, if not more direct, transformative opposition to the social systems in which we live. The study of these literatures and their pre-histories is important in itself; it is also important in understanding the U.S. and its literary culture, as well as relations to Latin America. What is more, the literatures may help in understanding the future of a significant sector of the U.S. workforce, as well as of the so-called "underclass," if conditions and prospects don't improve rapidly as we move toward the twenty-first century. While questions persist about the relation between Latino literature and the Latino social processes and cultural transformations they are supposed to represent, nevertheless it may said with some confidence that by projecting imaginatively and by not always respecting existing literary categories or fashions (to say nothing of respecting the normative grids applied in most social science research), at least some Latino literary works may come closer to expressing the deeper levels of Latino processes and transformations,

Latino patterns of accommodation and resistance, than do most conceptually driven historical and sociological approaches. This may give special social value not only to the works, but also to the growing corpus of Latino cultural and literary theory and criticism which provides means for understanding the creative works.

This essay attempts to contribute to the understanding of U.S. Latino literature by exploring some dimensions of Latino culture-in-transformation, and then some historical and theoretical aspects of Latino literary production, as a means of introducing the extended bibliography which follows.

II. LATINOS AND THEIR CULTURE

A. Identity.

Who are the Latinos, the Hispanos? How did they get here, what are their customs and beliefs? In what ways are they so similar and yet different from non-latinos and also from each other? Are there really any Latinos or Hispanos in the U.S., or are there only Mexicans, Puerto Ricans, Cubans, etc., lumped together for bureaucratic or political reasons but really very different.

And why "Latinos" "hispanos," "ibero-americanos," "hispanics," "Hispanic, Hispano, Latin or Ibero Americans?" Why can't they get together and agree on one name, one identity? Aren't they just being complicated to give us problems? And why do they claim to be different from Irish, Italian, Jewish or African Americans? Why don't they learn English?

Of course, most Latinos do learn English, and many of the questions asked and answers usually given are based on misconceptions. Most in fact do learn English, but there are so many recent arrivals that it seems not to be the case. The answers aren't easy in part because the questions may be misguided. And this problem has roots in the diversity and complexity of the Latino world. Many come from urban situations in the big cities. Others identify with temporal migrations and with life in small Texas towns. Some have had a history in what is today considered U.S. territory, for several generations; others arrived in the 1920s, the 40s, or a few weeks ago, from a poor region of Mexico, from a revolutionary struggle in Central America, from arid or tropical climates, from Afro- or Indian-Latin American areas or cultures, etc. Some in fact are more black, more Indian, more white than others, and there is no necessary connection between color or physical traits and cultural characteristics. Above all, to speak of *los hispanos* in the U.S. is to speak about key sectors of the work force, sectors that participated in industrial development and now participate with difficulty in the post-industrial process.

Latinos have so well served as a lowpaid work force in the railroads, the fields, restaurants and the wartime frontlines. Of course many Latinos work with their hands, and there are more and more who are professionals or business people; so we may ask if we are dealing with a people or various peoples with certain things in common that relate them to each other, but with such clear differences that we may wonder, again, if we should really be able to lump them together under one rubric.

Finally, Latinos may turn the issue around and ask, who are the *Americans*? When Latinos say, hey, I'm American, they may mean, look, I was born here or I have papers. But they can also be reminding us of the fact that every one in the new world is indeed American--that the word *American* doesn't only designate the people of (or "made in") the U.S.A.--and that in fact those who are often called "Americans" (and who have unwittingly or not appropriated the name of the entire continent) are also the only people in the Americas without a name that is totally and uncontestedly theirs. Then we come to the effort to find a name for all the Latin Americans living in the U.S.--those of the U.S. of Spanish language, culture or name. Again, who are they?

B. *Some Definitions*

I use the word *latino* rather loosely, to refer to people of Ibero-American birth or family origin who have been born in or who have, willingly or otherwise, come to see the U.S. as their home. *Latinos* manifest U.S. transformations of identities formerly achieved through a syncretic process in Latin America (including the U.S. southwest) itself. There is a traditionalist and generally conservative vision that defines Latinos strictly in function of their traditional language and cultural patterns; another anti-traditionalist and anti-culturalist vision, fostered by Werner Sollors and his followers[1], sees Latinos as products of the U.S. milieu. The option here is for a definition rooted in the work of Raymond Williams[2], which involves dialectical transformations of past cultural residues and future possibilities--which Juan Flores and George Yúdice conceptualize in terms of "crossovers" in postmodern, multicultural contexts (see Part IV of this essay). According to this view the achieved cultural *mestizaje* of Latin Americans and especially a workingclass dimension of this identity, which corresponds to the vast majority of those who come and settle in the U.S., undergoes a series of experiences and transformations leading to a range of shared behaviors and attitudes which in turn become the pool of characteristics from which given Latino groups and individuals constitute particular selections and combinations.

In recent years, we have come to employ the term *hispanic*, and in fact it is now the word that is used most frequently in legal documents and the press. But while many "hispanos" accept the word and reject other alternatives, including the one advanced here, there are still many "hispanos" who reject that name and, in fact, prefer the term "latino." Why? Most importantly, because they feel that the words *hispano*, *hispanic*, *Spanish*, etc., have to do with the Anglo effort to patronize Latinos--to say, "Oh, you are really a white European... Oh you are not like the others. That is, that you are hispanic, but not 'spic.'" In sum, Hispanic has come to prominence as a kind of left-hand compliment, by standing for "Spanishness"--that is, white, Europeanness, even if a kind of exotic brand. The word "hispanic" comes to suggest, then, the intent to erase (like a courtesy) the indigenous and African roots of Latin American identity. Given this hegemonic effort (in which many Latinos cooperate unconsciously and consciously), we have the contrary struggle for the name Latino.

Paradoxically the term has come to connote the product of Latin-

---

[1]Werner Sollors, *Beyond Ethnicity: Consent and Descent in American Culture* (NY: Oxford U. Press, 1986). See also Félix Padilla, *Latino Ethnic Consciousness: The Case of Mexican Americans and Puerto Ricans in Chicago* (Notre Dame, IN: Notre Dame U. Press, 1985).

[2]Cf. Williams, *The Sociology of Culture* (NY: Schocken, 1981).

Indian and/or Latin-African mestizaje. It has also come to evoke that other negativity, U.S.-based Latin American working class. I suppose in some Anglo minds, it conjures up *machismo*, black hair, gold crosses on chains, beaded curtains, tropical music, etc. But however pejorative or affirmative in connotation, the word "Latino" suggests a broad and aged otherness to Anglo American modernized norms--but an otherness constituted as almost an absence within the Western episteme. It suggests ethnic pride and cultural affirmation, not the hiding of black and brown blood that is implicit in the "Hispanic" label. Thus the term expresses paradox, complexity and defiance. It has come to stand for an affirmation of a struggle against racism, sexism and classism. It is to fight for the survival of the very language which was initially that of the colonizers and which now stands in resistance to the new powers-that-be. It is to affirm the workingclass base of the great majority of "Hispanics" in the U.S. It is to refuse cooperating with the racism, sexism and classism within Latinos themselves. It is to affirm Latin identity in contradistinction to an identity integrated with the dominant powers and their will to name and control.

Of course there is an ancient logic in the term, that has to do with the Roman Empire, Romance languages, the religion and even the law of Rome. But to use the term "Latino" today is to affirm paradoxically the cultures and peoples dominated by Mediterranean civilization in its career throughout the New World. Paradoxically the term has come to connote the product of Latin-Indian and/or Latin-African cultural mix. But the word "Latino" suggests a broad and aged otherness to Anglo American modernized norms--yet an otherness within our hemispheric frame, an otherness that is part of a more general New World cultural sphere. It suggests ethnic pride and cultural affirmation, in Afro- and Amerindian cultural traditions in combination with a dominant Mediterranean, Iberian-based core.

Regularly the situation of Latinos may best be understood in terms of their problems in confronting an individualist and capitalist civilization with a culture based on communal and precapitalist forms. Here the stress falls on cultural aspects that have to do with attitudes and customs based on the importance of kinship as central to group organization and behavior. Of course the ensemble of Latino values must be viewed not only as a synthesis of "the Hispanic," but also of the indigenous and also of the African. However, even with the specifically Hispanic dimension, the emphasis must fall on Spanish

diversity, on North African roots and the role of semitic cul
and Jewish) in the formation of the attitudes that have to
concepts of tribe, of race, of honor, of kinship, of sex roles,
of property, of life, death and in general identity seen as community
and family-based.

A complex aspect of Latino unity has been the retention of characteristics drawn from the cultural past that have been defined as "pre-capitalist," "early capitalist," "pre-industrial," "Catholic," "agrarian," "Spanish," "dependent," etc. It has been argued that these characteristics render Latinos as relatively "dysfunctional," "underprivileged" or "underdeveloped" within the rationalized productive system governing U.S. society; but they may well prove to be a source of strength against the more corrosive effects of material and technological advance. In fact, a more humane future for all people may well depend in part on the conservation of such "residual" characteristics among the Latinos and the "Latinization" of non-Latinos. However symptomatic of liberation, such matters as the rising rate of Latino divorce, ruptures of the extended family, the pressures for higher degrees of individuation, independent female participation, etc., imply cultural and psychological difficulties for large numbers.

In this sense part of the problematic Latinos face in trying to survive and live creative lives within the U.S. system has to do with the "interface" of Latino values and orientations with Anglo-Saxon/capitalist civilization. Without doubt, many Latinos suffer because they carry with them values and attitudes that still express an older communitarian, agrarian and semi-feudal logic. And while there are many Latino computer experts, we understand that the mass of Latino workers have forms of life that more readily fit with pre- and not post-industrial patterns. And we also know that these forms of life (including forms of courtesy and Catholicism) fit perfectly well in the capitalist world, but as forms of an "underclass" in what we call the "dual labor market."

We know that the basic cultural norms don't have to do with Protestant or individual identity, but with social, communitarian and family forms of being. We know that honor and loyalty to one's compadre are forms that are out of fashion and that don't thrive in a world where cash and "rational self interest" rule. But we also know that in our world, there is a considerable attraction to Latino values, and the hope that certain dimensions survive and thrive--something that is not pure "rational" interest, not sun-worship, "land fetishism," or irrational blood loyalty, but something which goes beyond a mechanical order of clocks, gears and the logic of productive efficiency. So there are many who have an interest in *Latino* norms who are not Latinos. But we should not see this purely as a product of anti-modern nostalgia. There are many Latinos who feel that the effort to preserve Latino culture contributes to the maintenance of Latinos in situations of marginalization and poverty. And of course there are those who want the best of both worlds; they want to combine "the best of the Anglo with the best of the Latino." But there are still others who argue convincingly that the great majority of Latinos who lose their culture come to suffer from a process of uprooting that leaves them with the worst possibilities for surviving in the modern world. Above all, some of us persist in seeing that the survival of Latino traditions involves the survival of elements that can serve in forging a more fruitful future for Latinos and for every one.

In this sense, Latino culture is seen by some to stand as an alternative to our dominant cultural norms. But others see Latino identity acting as a positive category *within* our overall culture, providing some of the sources for the future.

C. Some Questions About the Future of Latinos

Latino culture requires differentiation from other U.S. minority or ethnic cultures, and from strictly immigrant complexes, first because of the long-standing Indian, Mexican and Puerto Rican presence within territory directly taken by the U.S.; second, because of the fact of a common border between the U.S. and Mexico; third, because of the special legal status of Puerto Ricans and Cubans; and finally, because of the long-term and continuous two-way migratory pattern between the U.S. and Mexico, the U.S. and Puerto Rico. While immigration is a crucial matter, however, the main source of Latino population growth is still from the continued expansion of the existing U.S. Latino population pool.

Inevitably when we contemplate the growing Latino population, we immediately face questions of diversity and apparent disunity which prevent our overestimating the statistical growth: the U.S. Latino population does not automatically form a *bloc*; and even among many sectors with similar objective interests, it is extremely difficult to construct an effective unity. It is also hard to anticipate all the possible implications of the growth of the Latino population for the future. In spite of the new immigration policies, we can be sure that the flow will continue, because its causes will continue to be acute. The new efforts at free trade, even if successful for some, may not stem but may in fact intensify the reasons for immigration.

The obvious point to make is about problems Latinos may face in the future. First, there is the question of racism and cultural hostility, patterns of prejudice and discrimination, struggles with other minority groups--and all the rest. This is especially important when we realize that Latinos will potentially constitute a significant proportion of the workers employed or not in the country, and therefore that what happens to Latinos will be important for the future of the U.S. and for every one.

On first sight, the prospects can appear negative enough. Indeed, without some dramatic transformations and radical changes in state and corporate policies, current trends would lead to a situation in which a vast and growing population of unskilled, poorly educated workers functionally illiterate in Spanish and English, would be inserted in a society based on advanced technology and capital-intensive labor; we would have a population needing housing, social services, education and jobs in a nation whose own logic of development may well leave it ill-prepared to deal with its deepest problems. Indeed, since the median age of this population mass would be significantly lower than the U.S. majority, the nation would face an extenuation of an already existing polarization between an older, mainly white population (though with some strategic Latino intermediaries) which increasingly monopolizes wealth, resources and power, and a younger, mainly non-white population numerically dominated by Latinos, who will be waging an ever more difficult struggle to maintain and win access to institutions and resources in which the majority has lessening interest and commitment.

In this context, Latinos will have great socio-economic and political difficulties, but the cultural and psychological problem may be greater, as pressures affect family patterns and values, on sex roles, on all relations and identifications.

The question of a world of gangs and drugs, of the informal economy, of continuing and extending anomie, of dropouts and welfare dependency, of growing parental absenteeism, growing and deepening racial and gender conflicts, and the like have prevented Latino groups and others from uniting in the most meaningful ways. Now the world rolls on to the beat of postmodern, post-industrial logic and those who can't go with the flow and who can't get with the new world order are doomed to live on the margins, unable to adjust or react creatively to new transformations, and only able to hold on to the most questionable aspects of the older culture--precisely those which may best conform to, and then lend themselves to becoming transformed, by the logic of the informal economy and underclass patterns. The results may well be the "marginalization" of many, at the same time that some Latinos will rise to high positions of prestige and respect.

III. U.S. LATINO LITERATURE: HISTORY AND DEVELOPMENT

A. Latino Populations and Three Phases of Migration Literature

Popular impressions aside, the core base of U.S. Mexican population derives not from the northward migration of people from south of the border, but from the southward and westward migration of the border itself. To this day, in spite of great waves of immigration, the bulk of Mexican-descent population growth is from birth as opposed to immigration patterns. However, in addition to the Mexican population made part of the U.S. by wars of conquest, Mexican and then Mexican *tejano* migration became a major aspect of the U.S. Mexican population base, beginning early in the twentieth century, during the Mexican Revolution, in relation to the demand for labor on the railroads, in the fields, and of course in the steel mills, canning, food-processing and meatpacking plants of the midwest. Through ups and downs, periods of mass deportations and expanding immigration, that population base continued to grow, and to be joined after World War II by a major Puerto Rican exodus--and then by Cubans, significant numbers from the Dominican Republic, Ecuador, Colombia, Chile and elsewhere.

To be sure, many Puerto Ricans, Cubans and others came to the east coast, and especially to New York, in the late nineteenth century. But the Puerto Rican exodus intensified after the U.S. took the island in 1898 and especially after the developmentalist projects culminating in "Operation Bootstrap" pushed many people off the land and sent them first to San Juan, and then New York and other U.S. points in a search for work and survival. Of course the major waves of Cuban migration came immediately after the Revolution of 1959 and the exodus from the port of Mariel in 1980. Finally, since in recent years, growing numbers of Guatemalans, Salvadorans and Nicaraguans fleeing the political and economic crises in their respective countries have added to a core Mexican-Puerto Rican-Cuban population base which continues to expand because of high birth rates and homebase economic hardships throughout the decade.

Although heterogenous, the Mexican and Puerto Rican migrations were primarily workingclass, and the groups brought with them those elements of their national and Latin American culture, oral tradition and literature available to their social class and situations. For a distinct U.S. Latino culture and literature to emerge for each group in each locale, there had to be a sufficient experience of U.S. life, culture and language, to pressure Latin American cultural norms, and there had to be a sufficient degree of critical consciousness, generated through hardship, but articulated through institutional or extra-institutional/counter-cultural formations to make writing as a vehicle of cultural definition both necessary and possible. Obviously that literary expression required an adequate pooling of resources for at least minimal cultural reproduction and distribution--from self-publishing to small chapbook and literary journal production. To the degree that each emergent work of literature tended to stand in relation to broader cultural, literary and socio-psychological patterns, that work tended to follow certain general lines of "mainstream" or minority literary development dominant nationally; but the work was also marked by certain characteristics specific to its place and group of generation. This meant that each expression by each member of a national group was at least in part filtered through a particular, sometimes regional, sometimes even a more local sense of Latino identity.

Clearly the resources available would affect literary production, as would the specific characteristics of Latino populations in given areas. But, leaving aside the Latin American literature written by professionals who have come to the U.S. as part of the brain drain, U.S. Latino literature may be divided into two major categories, (1) a literature based on and extending from long ingrained indigenous U.S. southwest homebase traditions, and (2) a literature based on the experience of those many primarily working class people who have migrated from Mexico, Puerto Rico, and other parts of Latin America to the U.S.

during the course of the twentieth century. To be sure many of the people of the first group have virtually become part of the second by a dislocation process which has uprooted them from their Southwest homes and sent them to work and sometimes to settle in other parts of the country, so that their original cultural and literary base, rooted in 18th and 19th century traditions, has been influenced, affected and at least partially merged with the newer immigrant populations, which they have in turn also influenced. And to the degree that much of the U.S. Latino population has been one in transformation, we may consider that population's literary expression as being loosely divided into three phases, through which various population strands, generations and individuals have passed through at given historical moments.

The first phase is a romantic literature attempting to replicate the homebase literary culture (whether in the Southwest or Latin America) with variations in subjects, emphases and expressive modes deriving from the particularities of the writer's origins and experience, especially as the forces of "cultural shock" and transformation begin taking their toll. This usually means a nostalgic, nationalistic poetry of loss and exile, romantic, rhetorical and declamatory in style with conventional rhythms, rhyming patterns and poetic techniques. Mexican and border-area *corridos*, Puerto Rican *plenas* and other musical forms influence this literary expression, as do folklore, sayings, proverbs, etc.

The second phase is a literature of migration or immigration, marked by hopes, but also by problems, presenting everyday life confusions, conflicts, etc., frequently exploring racism and ethnic or national identity, an affirmation of roots, appeals to justice and envisioned social solutions. This literature emerges in all genres (in song, poetry, fiction and drama), but it tends to favor poetry at first and then begin to veer toward the development of more extended dramatic or narrative forms, modeled on, but varying from the early primary ones probably because of the complex and ever shifting experiences the forms attempt to encapsulate and articulate. At first this literature is only somewhat mediated by existing literary norms. It is performative, social, didactic, hortatory; it is often bitter, militant, defiant. Still close to oral roots, it may play far better than it reads. It is meant to be read and heard, by targeted groups in specific settings. In poetry, this is a literature often without rhyme, jagged in rhythm, imitating and extending from first older and then emergent musical forms, with some influences based on forms stemming from Afro-American, Native

American or other minority cultures. It is populist in orientation; but overtly or surreptitiously, in tone, gender-centering and ideology, its populism, democratic spirit and resistive counter-culturalism or otherness emerge within a patriarchal frame.

The third phase is a literature of settlement, also looking back on the homebase and immigration, but from a more settled-in framework, with an existing Latino tradition behind it, now reaching out to other minority and mainstream (U.S. mainly but also Latin American, African, etc.) to expand horizons and move either to pan-Latin American, "pan-third world" or U.S. mainstream identifications. Here the culture itself becomes self-critical and de-centered from earlier male discourse; feminist and post-nationalist issues become crucial, as do a wide range of alternative cultural models and directions. Expression is frequently more individual, subjective, inward; style replaces a generalized rhetoric. In one sense this literature may be an expression of assimilation or acculturation that may or may not represent the broader group aggregate (but rather a sector thereof); however, it may also be a literature which draws on, even as it critically distances itself from, earlier norms and suppositions.

These literatures are far from exclusive. Tendencies exist along a continuum. For example, in the Midwest, Latino literature develops late when overall U.S. Latino consciousness and literature is moving along the continuum from the second to the third phase. Even as new versions of older modes reappear in relation to recent immigration and development patterns, contemporary midwest Latino literature tends to telescope the second and third phases to produce a literature which may still have roots in the rural land, or a *barrio* or colonia surrogate, but which tends to project beyond national to broader Latino and universal concerns. And the multi-layered and diverse urban environments of our literary centers make it possible for a single writer to go through all three phases in a matter of a few years.

What follows is a brief overview of the main developments and characteristics of Chicano, Puerto Rican and other Latino literatures in the U.S.

B. The Development of Chicano Literature

Mexican literature has existed in the territory which is now the U.S. as long as there have been Mexicans--that is, from the time of the Spanish settlements in what is now the Southwest. Indeed, what we today call Chicano literature is really, first a Southwest variant of Mexican literature and then an emergent immigrant literature written by the successive waves of twentieth century immigrants and especially their second and third generation offspring. Of course, new immigrants have continued to arrive, almost completely ignorant of the history and cultural production of those who arrived in U.S. territory before them (immigrants of the 1980s have little knowledge about or at least initial interest in the Chicano movement of the 1960s, to say nothing of the cultural and literary production that movement spurred). But tendencies toward what we today consider Chicano, as opposed to Mexican, literature, begin to emerge in the Southwest even in the nineteenth century and on into our own time.

A few nineteenth century writers, as well as some of the early writers of *corridos* and theatrical skits, and then, a few figures like Daniel Venegas in our own century, are among the first to move from an initial Mexican base (in U.S. Southwest or specifically national Mexican terms) to a new Chicano literature which begins to dwell on the U.S. experience, the clash of old and new cultural trends, the pressures on language and identification, the problems of cultural loss, prejudice, discrimination, poverty and urban blight.

Clearly a Chicano ethnic folk literature developed in the Southwest and continues to find varied modern expression in a Rudolfo Anaya or Sabine Ulibarrí. There is of course a literature of regional life and family sagas, as in Hinojosa's *Klail City Death Trip*, Nash Candelaria's cycle of novels or Victor Villaseñor's recent *Rain of Gold*. But there is a more urban-based strand, the precursors of which are writers like Venegas, which portrays the problems of modern "*barrio* life" and the effort to defend identity through the concern with "roots" and the elaboration of a mythic source of identity-structure such as that which developed during the heydays of the Chicano movement with the concept of *Aztlán*. Poets such as José Montoya, J.L. Navarro, Raúl Salinas, Abelardo Delgado and Ricardo Sánchez were among the first to portray the modern *barrio* in a rhetorical poetry of revelation and protest; while novelists as José Villarreal, Richard Vásquez and Alejandro Morales presented portraits of Chicano urban life. With poet Alurista and playwright Luis Valdez of *El Teatro Campesino*, Chicano literature became centered on *Aztlán* as the lost promised land which must be recaptured and maintained at least in spirit if Chicanos were to survive the pressures of what many of them saw as a soulless and racist technocratic order which threatened to devour them.

From efforts to reclaim land grants to the symbolic positing of a pre-Colombian mystical realm, Chicano writers developed the concept of *Aztlán* as a pre-capitalist, land and spirit-centered basis for Chicano culture, literature and political activity. Even as Chicano literature developed throughout the 1960s and 1970s and on into the 1980s, even as new Chicano writers showed new levels of sophistication, left older modes of protest and incorporated new Latin American and U.S. models as the bases for their developing work, the *Aztlán* myth or one of its variations as a "sacred space" would still tend to characterize Chicano literature and serve as its paradigm, only to be eroded by the more secular, rationalist and feminist trends that would emerge increasingly in the 1980s as a literature of settlement and acculturation began to displace the older cultural model for many writers.

No more provocative formulation of the pre- or anti-capitalist/anti-modern, land-centeredness of Chicano literature, and no better means to understand different Chicano works and trends against national norms and currents has been suggested, than the post-structuralist paradigm elaborated in relation to Chicano poetic discourse by critic Juan Bruce-Novoa in the 1970s and given most complete articulation, variation and elaboration (from paradigm to anti-paradigm) in his *Retro-Space* (1990).

For Bruce-Novoa, the surface concerns of Chicano literature point to a "deep structure" based on the loss of a world, or "*axis mundi*" and an effort to recuperate the lost world through some kind of creative recreation of space. This paradigm is played out in function of the polarities of life and death. Its deeper, anthropological roots may be found in a tribal sense of communal, sacred space. One is only alive in relation to a community which occupies and defines that space. Exiled, one enters the land of death, a world of chaos in which the "center will not hold," the spiritual disorder which is the modern experience, or the world of time as opposed to spatial values, chronometric/labor time as opposed to sun/space time: the world not of maize, but of money and machines.

As Bruce-Novoa argues, Chicano literature is the space of symbolic action between the forces of "life and death" in relation to the disappearance, survival and transformation of the Mexican *axis mundi*. Each progressive historical transformation of the *axis mundi* implies what Bruce-Novoa describes as the "erasure" (or conservation even in negation) of what is formally canceled. It is the Conquest which marks a major rupture in the violation of the *axis mundi*. The Independence and future Mexican struggles represent efforts by varying groups to "erase the erasure" and retake the Mexican space.

The threat of group obliteration intensifies in the modern world of displacement from the countryside, of migration, migrant labor and cross border immigration. Mexico is canceled by migration and displacement. A whole value world and cosmology is lost. The people try to reconstruct the sacred in their new space, the *colonia*, *barrio* or street, only to find this space and the people attacked from without and threatened by disintegration from within, with only certain possibilities for survival and reconsecration, to be found in those who, while valuing change, take on older roles of incanting the wise and magic words and enacting the proper rituals. The new turf becomes the new Chicano *axis mundi* to be held and defended, as the U.S. experience cuts the people off from Mexico and as Mexico cuts them off from the U.S. window onto the world. But the *barrio* is a fallen Mexican world, one in which there seem to be few creative avenues, in which what is left of cultural roots may hem one in and hold one down, more than provide modes of liberation. Indeed, defense of the sacred turf may lose all significant cultural reference as it synchronizes with or rather becomes reduced to generalized "underclass" or even gang orientations.[3] The question then becomes how to find creative resolution, how to protect oneself from the identity chaos of the external world, but how on the other hand not to be trapped by what from that internalized external world's point of view is the prison of a traditional culture which no longer holds even the illusions of rewards and possibilities that it formerly offered.

The artist is seen as a kind of shaman, recreating the communal space or its surrogates and winning a war against invading forces of chaos. Of course one frequently must take on the enemy's tactics and weapons; one cannot strictly bring back the old. You cannot restore old Mexico or bring back *Aztlán*, but you can win creative space ritual-

---

[3] For a view based on Chicago's Pilsen barrio, see Ruth Horowitz, *Honor and the American Dream: Culture and Identity in a Chicano Community* (New Brunswick: Rutgers U. Press, 1983).

istically, artistically, through creative reconstruction and projection. The space of the printed page becomes the communal writer's space of victory.

Clearly, this kind of cosmology has ties to the evocations of structural transformations specified in the writings of Octavio Paz; as a sophisticiated reformulation of the *Aztlán* construct and theme so central to Chicano cultural and literary mythology, this orientation has been subjected to intense critique as constituting an overly normative definition of Chicano literature. Interestingly, Bruce-Novoa himself has been intensely involved in the critical and deconstructive process.

Sixties Chicano literary editors and critics castigated or ignored Chicano writers to the degree that they did not write an ethnic, Chicano literature in terms similar to those we have established here. Thus writers like Tomás Rivera and, even more so, Rudolfo Anaya, were set up as models, and seemingly non-ethnic writers like John Rechy were relegated to a closet they did not wish to inhabit. In a classic instance, it is alleged that pioneering Chicano editor Herminio Ríos even excluded at least one story from Rivera's novel, ...*y no se lo tragó la tierra*, on the grounds that the story gave too negative an image of Chicanos. The major contemporary Latino editor, Nicolás Kanellos has attacked the ethnic immigrant narrative as an exhausted paradigm and, it is said, guided young writers to tone down its presence through the selection process for the collections of their work; and Bruce-Novoa has become an absolute champion of canon reform.[4] But this reform has prompted continual theoretical interventions, such as the major one we find in Ramón Saldívar's recent *Chicano Narrative: The Dialectics of Difference* (1990), and in a variety of other, and especially feminist, critics and writers.

More overtly political than Bruce-Novoa, Saldívar uses an interdisciplinary, critical methodology involving the Derrida's deconstructionism and Fredric Jameson's conceptualization of a "political unconsciousness" to portray Chicano literature as a part of, yet resistant to the mainstream of, U.S. literature, and to characterize it as struc-

---

[4]See their articles in Lavonne Ruoff and Jerry W. Ward, Jr., eds. *Redefining American Literary History* (New York: Modern Language Association, 1990), as well as Bruce-Novoa's *RetroSpace*.

turing oppositional differences with respect to both hegemonic Anglo-American literary, cultural and ideological norms and the evolving socio-economic and political processes to which they are related. By this account, deconstructionism operates to undermine the binary oppositions which seemingly structure discourse in the production of differential textual meaning. This procedure opens textual structuration to interpretations based on Jameson's conceptualization of relations between Marxist concerns such as production, class and transformative action and Freudian views of such phenomena as tied to neurosis-producing repression and sublimated expression. Basing his analysis on dialectical, socially rooted difference, Saldívar sees Chicano narrative as involving deconstructions of imposed Anglo identities for the production of literary meaning. Interpretation of literary texts means understanding the relationship of their symbolic patterns to their generic conventions and the broader social and political forces which writers internalize and express through processes such as those Freud identified in his treatment of the unconscious.

Whereas Chicano narrative may have seemed less overtly oppositional than other literary modes, Saldívar underlines its varieties of difference as they articulate themselves in relation to existent generic norms and variations which mediate between given literary works and the social world they would seem to represent. Thus, Chicano reactions to Anglo American racism initially found expression in the border corrido, which solidified in the second half of the nineteenth century and then experienced successive transformations and pressures until it gave way to other expressive forms under the weight of historical change. Modern urban Chicano poetry is one mode developing out of and varying the corrido frame. But the varying novelistic forms which emerge at the time of the Chicano movement constitute the primary mode of Chicano expression in the period extending from the 1960s to present.

Most of the major Chicano narratives of the 1960s and 1970s, no matter how varying in formal experimentation, were in fact male *bildungsroman*, so that the emergence of women writers and feminist narratives in the 1980s meant a constitution of works that were multiply differential and resistant, in that they went counter not only to the hegemonic culture, but also to the Chicano patriarchal patterns and even the mainstream feminism which sought to oppose that culture.

Recent Chicana feminist ideologues like Norma Alarcón, Gloria Anzaldúa and Cherríe Moraga have articulated a new oppositional stance by rewriting Chicano male-centered macro-mythologies in terms of feminist ones which question all fixity of gender/race/class identities and norms; meanwhile Chicana feminist fiction writers have sought to explore the micro-world of everyday life patternings to find the multiple modes of possible resistances within the seams of lived experience and creative projection.

Now, under the impact of deconstructionism, feminism, postmarxism and other postmodernist modes of thought, much contemporary Chicano writing male and female seeks to break through beyond earlier narrow ethnic concerns to ones which require new modes of understanding and analysis to grasp how the writing maintains or transcends earlier patterns and identifications. The new writing is inevitably more urban, more closely woven with other Latino and non-Latino cultural strains, more distanced from a pre-technological, pre-capitalist world of blood bonds and sacrifices, sacramental, ritualistic and ceremonial relations with the earth and other humans; it is also distanced from the world of confrontational violence with Rangers, cops or rival gangs.

In line with the educational circumstance achieved by at least a sector of Chicanos in U.S. life, writers like Gary Soto, Alberto Ríos and several others are increasingly characterized by their withdrawal from Chicano ethnic literature and from the culturalist paradigm early identified with it. As for the feminist Chicana writers, Helena María Viramontes, Denise Chávez, as well as Ana Castillo and Sandra Cisneros, seem to drift both from Bruce-Novoa's spatial identification or Saldívar's construction of machistic border and barrio defiance; they struggle ambivalently with the older paradigms as well as the repression and the inscribed role of women which they find as central to them and to at least certain dimensions of the Chicano movement they have been seen to represent. Still others, like Cecile Piñeda, Shiela Ortiz Taylor and Laurence Gonzales (cf. his *4-4-4* [Columbia, MO: University of Missouri Press, 1977]) seem fully turned toward the mainstream without struggling with the older paradigms or being particularly centered on them.

Nevertheless, in one way or another, many contemporary Chicano writers, and especially male ones, directly or indirectly, consciously or not, project the early paradigmatic Chicano vision into contemporary settings and circumstances; and it may well be that contemporary feminist work, as well as other "new wave"-tending Chicano literature can still be shown to partake, however critically, of a land-centered structural view as a necessarily regressive, pre-capitalist oppositional mode, now refashioned to project a more progressive, late capitalist resistant pattern. If this is the case, then we would still be able to establish the core ties of Chicano writers to a vision which is very specifically rooted in a syncretic "imaginary" where Mexican and U.S. polarities find their resolution. We would still be able to speak of a specifically "ethnic" literature, rather than a general literature written by writers who just happen to be Chicano.

This orientation may continue to have importance if we believe that even the enforcement of the new immigration laws cannot resist the pressure created by circumstances in Mexico, and that, even as we have new generations of sophisticated Chicanos able to read and absorb the sophisticated writings of new writers, we will continue to have large, new Chicano social sectors who must find or create a literature expressive of and suited to their own situation and experience.

C. *Puerto Rican Literature in the U.S.*

Without question, the most famous writer of Puerto Rican descent in the United States was the doctor-poet, William Carlos Williams, who, Puerto Rican on his mother's side, apparently disassociated himself from the cultural traditions of the island, even after his visits there and his translations of poetry by Luis Palés Matos. Only today are critics taking seriously his Puerto Rican and Latin roots as a means of understanding his similarities and differences with other New World writers.[5] The lack of recognition of Williams' own "Puerto Rican"

---

[5] See Yanis Gordils, "Island and Continental Puerto Rican Literature: Cross-Cultural and Intertextual Considerations," *ADE Bulletin*, no. 91 (Winter 1988), pp. 54; her source, Julio Marzán, "Mrs. Williams's William Carlos," *Latin American Literature: Reinventing the Americas*, ed. Bell G. Chevigny and Gari Laguardia (NY: Cambridge U. Press, 1986), pp. 106-21; and Vera Kutzinski, *Against the American Grain: Myth and History in William Carlos Williams, Jay Wright, and Nicolás Guillén* (Baltimore: Johns Hopkins U. Press, 1987), pp. 37 and 258.

identity may be taken as a sign for the broader series of questions having to do with the recognition of Continental Puerto Rican writing as part of U.S. and U.S. Latino literature and also as part of Puerto Rican literature. What follows mainly has to do with the first question, but the second one is also important to consider.

Some years ago, in his introduction to an anthology of U.S. Puerto Rican poetry, Efraín Barradas went to great lengths to point out the lack of continuity and community between Nuyorican and Island writers.[6] One of the most difficult tasks in explaining U.S. Puerto Rican writing is to *distinguish* between island-oriented literature (even when it is written in New York and/or is about the U.S. diaspora), which is a branch of Caribbean or Latin American literature, and Continental U.S. Puerto Rican writing which, no matter where written, at least tends to be a U.S. ethnic literature. In attempting to make a bridge between island and Continental expression, we cannot overlook the differences, which have been felt so keenly by those on both sides of the divide.

Because of his genuine concern with unity, Barradas refuses to evade the differences and their bases in fact. Above all, he notes the tendency of "Nuyorican" writers toward heretical demythifications and/or mythmaking constructs with respect to Puerto Rican culture and national identity. Obviously the reasons for these constructs lie in the root causes for the immigration of Puerto Ricans to New York: the island's colonial status and the economic upheaval caused by efforts of modernization, and of course the very negative and demoralizing circumstances most Puerto Ricans have encountered in the U.S. So we have a mythifying of the island and a search for alternative role models and identifications; and we have, above all, the assertion of an injured, denied and hence defiant sense of national and cultural pride.

At times, continental Puerto Ricans have resisted dealing with themselves as a U.S. minority, because to do so would imply a negation of a focus on their island's colonial status. Even as unemployment,

---

[6]Barradas, "Introducción" to *Herejes y mitificadores: Muestra de Poesía puertorriqueña en los estados unidos*, ed. Efraín Barradas and Rafael Rodríguez (Rio Piedras, Puerto Rico: Ediciones Huracán, 1980), p. 11.

poor housing, drug and welfare dependency, gang and school dropout rates, etc., became increasingly endemic in the Puerto Rican community, such problems could only be seen as legitimate to the degree that they were subsumed in function of the situation of Puerto Ricans as a colonized people. And the entire immigration process, seen from the island intelligentsia's struggle to preserve a fragile, jeopardized national identity, could only be construed as loss. This sense of loss, felt in the very bones by those having their base in a U.S. enclave, and unable to recapture fully their island roots, has led to sometimes desperate alternatives--from a fullblown romanticism with respect to the island, to a rejection of the island and a search for other worlds.

Indeed, perhaps for their smaller numerical size as a population (or as a tiny writer/artist subculture), and perhaps also for the fragility and difficult-to-specify character of their sense of nationhood, U.S.-based Puerto Rican writers, more than their Mexicano counterparts, tended to decenter or go beyond national identification to Latino and third world/minority identifications even to the degree that they affirmed their nationhood. So, the first Puerto Rican writers in the U.S. learned to project their visions of island independence in terms of union with Cuba and the broader Caribbean world. And, in this century, it is no accident that in Chicago, where the Puerto Rican population exists in the context of a much larger Mexican presence, the major contribution to the developing national scene was *Revista Chicano-Riqueña*, fathered by U.S. Rican Nicolás Kanellos.

While recent Chicano writers have attacked, abandoned or transformed the *Aztlán* construct as the armature for their poetic explorations, the problem for Puerto Rican writers has been the elaboration of a series of partial, fragmented mythologies in the face of a lack of an abiding and binding ur-myth that could give depth and unity to the epiphenomenal thematics of their work. So the occasional and topical feel and at least appearance of much U.S. Puerto Rican writing, and also the tentative and melancholy nature of the writers' heresies and mythologies; so the apparently more limited volume and elaboration of Puerto Rican literature compared to the Chicano counterpart. This is the viewpoint articulated rather arrogantly in Bruce-Novoa's *Retro-Space*. But if there is some truth in this contrast, stemming as it does from the lost past of Caribbean cultures (as opposed to the at least partial continuities involved in Mexican history), and from a lack of longterm residence or rootedness (through workforce or proprietorial relatedness--through a standing as permanent workers, business people or homeowners) in a land which they have felt theirs by some deep and sacred pact (the case of at least some people living in the Southwest, and part of the mythic structuration of much Chicano literature), nevertheless, this very situation helps to define the profundity behind the sometimes superficial appearances.

We have in fact just designated "the space of U.S. Puerto Rican literature" as one primarily for the exploration and forging of a new sense of identity and nation in the face of loss and disorientation, multi-ethnicity and multi-Latino identifications, in the face of the loss of myths which is increasingly the postmodern condition for Chicanos just as for others in contemporary life. The space of this literature separates even as it relates it to Puerto Rican island writing; the space is where the Puerto Rican colony or *barrio* is related to the city and its majority and minority populations, to the island, the Caribbean, Africa and the world. Gender will also emerge as a concern. In this context, the main contribution of much recent Puerto Rican writing is the insistence we have pointed to on a broad Latin and even internationalist focus even in the midst of developments emphasizing U.S. Puerto Rican nationalist, broadly minority and feminist trends. And in this context too, the question emerges (in a way it hardly ever does for Puerto Rican island writers) about what may have been *gained* by Puerto Ricans in spite of the obvious negative dimensions of the diaspora.

To be sure, as our reference to William Carlos Williams assures, Puerto Rican literature in the continental U.S. does not begin with the Puerto Rican diaspora of economic refugees to New York. In a recent article, Juan Flores divides Puerto Rican literature to the U.S. into three phases, preceded by a kind of "pre-phase".[7]

The "pre-phase," extending from the last century consists of exiles from the independence struggle against Spain (major intellectuals like Hostos, Betances, etc., but also "a solid base of artisans and laborers"), who spent varied lengths of time in New York, forming Puerto Rican and Antillean independence support groups and writing mainly about

---

[7]Juan Flores, "Puerto Rican Literature in the United States: Stages and Perspectives," in *ADE Bulletin* no. 91, pp. 39-44 (and now in *Divided Borders*). His phases are an extension and refinement of Eugene Mohr's, in *The Nuyorican Experience* (see Annotations, VIII. C.).

their Caribbean struggles, but also (in the case of Hostos's diaries or the poetry of Francisco Gonzalo ["Pachín"] Marín) reflecting critically on the New York experience of arriving Puerto Rican nationals.

The first phase, extending from 1917 to 1945, is mainly of autobiographical and journalistic works expressing the efforts of first generation immigrants, many of them with the feelings and attitudes of foreign nationals and subject people (and here their difference from other immigrants), to adjust to U.S. life. This period is most fully and richly represented by *The Memoirs of Bernardo Vega* and Jesus Colón's *A Puerto Rican in New York and Other Sketches*. But, as Flores notes, it is also represented by fragments from a vast, still-accessible stream of oral history, and a still more accessible volume of popular music (boleros, plenas, etc.,) in which Rafael Hernández and other popular song writers expressed a wide range of feelings about the experience of Puerto Ricans coming to the city.

After the initial development of agro-business, industrialization efforts under Operation Bootstrap were responsible for the massive movement of poor, country Puerto Ricans off their land and into a migratory process that brought them to U.S. cities. The period of this migration, from 1945-65, constitutes the second phase of developing U.S. Puerto Rican literature. As immigrants, the Puerto Ricans of this period arrived too late to the feast of U.S. industrial expansion. Whereas many Mexicans, lacking legal status and having to take whatever job became available, gradually integrated themselves into the U.S. workforce (albeit in marginal roles), all too many Puerto Ricans, lacking adequate or marginal skills and suffering from cultural and racial discrimination as well, failed to find permanent niches in a declining industrial base; and, as U.S. citizens, they found their modes of survival in low-paying, tem-porary jobs, and (the subject of Oscar Lewis's notorious study of the "culture of poverty," *La Vida*), the famous U.S. systems of welfare and the "informal economy."

The circumstances of emergent lumpenization and what many saw as a loss of Puerto Rican/Latin American values and the attendant defense of the very system which was undoing them led to the emergence of two predominant literary modes. First, there was a very powerful, negative "view from the island"--a perspective focusing on the problems of workingclass Puerto Rican immigrants shared by writers whether living in San Juan or New York and represented most famously by Pedro Juan Soto, René Marquéz, Enrique Laguerre, José

Luis González and Emilio Díaz Varcárcel (this kind of writing continues into our own times with writers such as Iris Zavala, Iván Silén and Victor Fragoso).

Second, there was a "view from within the community" by a group of exile writers with long residence in New York (Clemente Soto Vélez and Julia de Burgos among them), writing mainly a literature of exile with hardly any bilingualisms and only limited reference (e.g., in Pedro Carrasquillo's *jíbaro décimas*) to the immigration experience--with only Guillermo Cotto-Thorner's novel, *Trópico en Manhattan*, and various works by Jaime Carrero turning toward the depth exploration of the immigration experience and the linguistic and cultural "*neorkismos*," which were to become common in the next stage of Puerto Rican literature.

This third, or Nuyorican stage of U.S. Puerto Rican literature "arose with no direct reference to or evident knowledge of the writings of the early period.... But nevertheless in prose at least [it] effectively draws together the firsthand testimonial stance of the 'pioneer' stage and the fictional, imaginative approach of the writers of the 1950s or 1960s" (Flores, p. 43). Clearly, this definition applies to such narratives of male becoming by Piri Thomas, Lefty Barreto, Nicky Cruz, Humberto Cintrón, Edwin Torres and Edward Rivera, as well as much of the work of the best known Nuyorican woman writer, Nicholasa Mohr--whose most famous narratives are, as Arnaldo Cruz-Malavé points out, "narratives of formation," or *bildungsromane* exploring the fate of outsiders caught often between one or more sets of conflictive polarities: Puerto Rico/New York, city/suburb, Latin culture/anglo culture, semifeudal patriarchism/capitalist feminism, etc.[8]

According to Cruz-Malavé, Puerto Rican writers have been most prolific in poetry, where, more than in other genres they have mapped out the polarities specified by Barradas between mythification and heretical demythification, which "constitute a dialectic that may be said to have its origins in the New York Puerto Rican awakening of the late 1960s" in the work of the Puerto Rican members of the Last Poets and

---

[8]Cf. Arnaldo Cruz-Malavé, "Teaching Puerto Rican Authors: Identity and Modernization in Nuyorican Texts," in *ADE Bulletin* no. 91, pp. 45-48. This essay is the main source for what follows here on Nuyorican poetry.

in a group known as the Young Lords (Cruz-Malavé: 48). Early Nuyorican poetry draws on militant Afro-American and Beat influences, as well as William Carlos Williams. It speaks for a community, more than an individual, and seeks to strip away false consciousness about the "American Dream" and Nuyorican colonial status in a third world ghetto; it seeks to promote action in the direction of nation-building.

Gradually Nuyorican writing becomes freer of prior models and develops its own voice, in the works of such writers as Pedro Pietri, Victor Hernández Cruz, Miguel Piñero, Miguel Algarín, Angel Figueroa, Tato Laviera and Martín Espada. Still tending to portray the New York ghetto world against a mythified view of a inter-racial utopia identified with a liberated Puerto Rico, these poets begin to break down the mythified strand and move in a richer, more complex frame of polarities and contradictions, which they portray not only in poetry but in plays as well. Indeed, for Miguel Algarín, by the mid-seventies, Nuyorican poetry had already developed three modes which he saw also as an overlapping continuum of phases in Nuyorican writing.[9] First there was "outlaw poetry," involving expressions of hostility, rage and violence; second, there was "evolutionary poetry," entailing a growing con-sciousness of the external determinations of outlaw moods and acts, as well as a movement toward transcendence; finally there was "dusmic poetry," tracing the transformation of aggression into spiritual strength, wholeness and freedom.

Even in Algarín's last phase, which parallels our view of the third stage of U.S. Latino literature in general, U.S. Puerto Rican literature does not leave specific national and ethnic considerations behind. So, in recent years, with Hernández Cruz's stylistic and thematic experiments and with the gender explorations of Sandra María Esteves, Luz María Umpierre, Judith Ortiz Cofer and others, we see new modes and new cultural horizons only hinted at fifteen years ago, but in no way signalling an end to Spanish, and collective orientations, in no way signifying accommodation or assimilation. Piñero is gone, but others have arrived. Ed Vega and others may parody the earlier immigrant narratives and may search for new narrative paradigms; but this, far

---

[9]Miguel Algarín, in his introduction to an anthology edited with Miguel Piñero, *Nuyorican Poetry: An Anthology of Puerto Rican Words and Feelings* (New York: William Morrow, 1975).

from signalling an end, just points to the fact that, in Tato Laviera's wonderful phrase, the *carreta* has been making a u-turn. So, in concluding his essay, Flores notes that, like Chicano and other "'minority' or non-canonical literatures of the United States," Continental Puerto Rican literature since its Nuyorican phase has been, while intensely national in orientation, also "a literature of recovery and collective affirmation, ... of 'mingling and sharing,' of interaction and exchange with neighboring, complementary cultures." However, while paying homage to Afro-American literature as influence and Chicano literature as cross-fertilizing parallel and presence, Flores adds that, most distinctively among these minority literatures, "Puerto Rican writing today is a literature of straddling, a literature operative within and between two national literatures and marginal in both. In this respect," he concludes, "Nuyorican writing may well come to serve as a model or paradigm for emerging literatures by other Caribbean groups in the United States, such as Dominicans, Haitians and Jamaicans" (Flores: 44).

Noting the broader perspective, Cruz-Malavé (50) argues that "Because of the diversity of the Puerto Rican experience, encompassing both the Third and First Worlds, underdevelopment and advanced capitalism, oral and written traditions," Puerto Rican writing has not just been a matter of survival stories and poems "in the fringes" of U.S. society, but "the space where ... the strategies for change--the many attempts to find a space of resistance and freedom outside (and inside) [First and Third World] modernization and [First World, late capitalist] consumerism--are taken to their ultimate consequences."

As we project to future phases of U.S. Puerto Rican literature, we should simply note that from the perspective of Chicago and the Midwest, the designation by Flores and Cruz Malavé (but not Barradas) of the third phase of Puerto Rican literature in the U.S. as "Nuyorican" is misleading, since it leaves out a significant area and all the other centers where the new literature developed. Future studies must include these other communities in and around New York, but the midwest as well--wherever Puerto Ricans have gone and will be going. In further efforts, and above all in developing a more sophisticated critique of the remarkably slow and limited emergence of a Puerto Rican woman's and specifically feminist literature, however, the perspectives specified above, will continue to serve as significant guideposts.

D. Cuban and Other U.S. Latino Literatures

As noted earlier in this brief study, the coming of Cubans, Dominicans, Central American and other Latin Americans to the U.S. has led to the emergence of new works, mainly in Spanish, expressive of their experience. To be sure, transplanted Cuban or Argentine novelists are not in any sense writing U.S. Latino literature, whether their characters twist and turn through Havana, Buenos Aires, Montevideo or New York. Only those writers representing groups with several years of U.S. residence and having had some working class as well as some *barrio* experience (including discrimination) are likely to write something which approaches community literary expression such as we find in U.S. Chicano and Puerto Rican literatures. An Argentine lawyer may write fiction in the mode of Borges or Cortázar; his or her daughter or son may outdo John Updike or Ann Tyler. But in either case, even if we find some residues, inflections, or specific "ethnic markings," the result will not necessarily be U.S. Latino literature.

Of all the groups mentioned, the Cubans certainly have had long enough residence and population density to produce a distinct ethnic literature in this country. And indeed the first steps in the development of U.S. Cuban writing tend to parallel the Puerto Rican model, in spite of initial historical and cultural differences. There is a pre-1898 phase, most famously represented by José Martí, that is virtually identical with that described by Juan Flores and summarized above. And, in spite of the differing immigration statuses allotted to inhabitants from the two islands in the wake of 1898, there was a similar development of U.S. Cuban writing throughout the first half of this century.

For the most part, Cuban immigration was never large or very permanent; and while tobacco workers migrated, many entering Cubans were from higher layers in Cuban society. Also, many politicized middle sector Cubans continued to come from the 1930s through the 1950s fleeing the regimes of Machado and Batista, some returning as new governments came to power. Still, small enclaves developed in New York and Miami, and their socio-cultural (not to say literary) history still requires study, if only because it will reveal the kinds of communities which opened the doors to the massive Cuban migration that arrived after Castro's coming to power.

Not surprisingly, what has tended to separate most Cubans and their literature in the U.S. from their Mexican and Puerto Rican cousins has been their predominantly middle class background (we refer here mainly to Cubans arriving before the Mariel exodus of 1980) and of course the political circumstances surrounding their departure from Cuba and their installation in Miami and other communities.

As Naomi Lindstrom has noted, U.S.-based Cubans have "apparently made few attempts to create a minority subculture literature such as that of Nuyoricans." Indeed, "typical of Cuban American production are the numerous works produced by anti-Castro Cubans" that are usually "right wing and conservative Catholic," and that "feature expressions of outrage ... , depictions of the sufferings of upper ... or middle-class families. [Here] the important elements are the continuity the authors see between Cuban culture as such and the culture they themselves represent in the act of writing.... Several bibliographic summaries group these writers not with other U.S. Hispanics, but with anti-Castro writers living ... elsewhere. Spanish is their literary language, and they seldom attempt to represent the effects of continual ... contact with ... English-speaking culture."[10]

This tendentious Cuban exile literature has its right and also left wing parallels in other Latin American groups based in the U.S. and across the globe. In fact, a current of exile literature developed during the 1960s among some of the children of the post-Castro exile identifying themselves as the *grupo Areíto* and seeking "dialogue" with Cubans on the island. Mainly writing in Spanish, but sometimes in English, leading group members like Lourdes Casal, Eliana Rivero and others created their works out of pained nostalgia and a desire for reconciliation, rebelling against their parents' politics but also against their pro-U.S. elitism and their unwillingness to see themselves in relation to other Latinos except when it was convenient. In the Areíto group, then, were seeds of a very different orientation not only toward Cuba but toward the U.S. experience--seeds that were to grow even af-

---

[10]Naomi Lindstrom, "Cuban and Continental Puerto Rican Literature," in David William Foster, ed., *Sourcebook of Hispanic Culture in the United States* (Chicago: American Library Association, 1982), pp. 224-225. In characterizing Cuban exile literature, Lindstrom draws on Seymour Menton, *Prose Fiction of the Cuban Revolution* (Austin: Institute for Latin American Studies, University of Texas, 1975), pp. 215-46; 305-8.

ter Casal's early death, in Rivero's continuing and expanding immersion in U.S. feminist writing as critic and poet. This U.S. orientation came to be shared by many other Cuban writers regardless of their stance vis-a-vis Cuban Communism. That is, increasingly albeit gradually, the sons and daughters of middle class Cuban families in the U.S. have begun to write a literature rooted in U.S. experience. And most of them have surpassed their U.S. Cuban forerunners in this regard.

Even among the tendentious exile writers there were some who did not fully ignore the U.S. experience as such. Some of the stories by Lino Calvo Novás, while haunted by the trauma of the Revolution, show a keen eye for aspects of life in Miami and New York. Octavio Armand, Isel Rivero, José Sánchez Boudy and Matías Montes Huidobro are four key writers who managed to write prose and poetry capturing major "ethnic" and "Latino" aspects of the U.S. Cuban situation. Armand in particular is important for his poetry, but also for his journal, *Escandalar*, a conduit for U.S. Cuban writing on displacement, loss, confusion and reidentification. Perhaps the most important traditional writer in this respect is Celedonio González, whose key works, *Los cuatro embajadores* (1973) and *El espesor del pellejo de un gato ya cadáver* (1978) deal with cultural shock and even the exploitation of Cuban workers.[11]

To be sure, during the 1960s, talented off-Broadway playwright María Irene Fornes had launched herself into the mainstream with little direct reflection of her Latino or Cuban roots--matters which only appear in her work during the 1980s. Then, a few years ago, another writer, Oscar Hijuelos, significantly a son of parents who immigrated to the U.S. in the 1940s, wrote a major example of Latino autobiographical fiction in his *Our House in the Last World*. But this book and many other Latino-tending Cuban works were examples of American Dream Romance too inadequate in oppositional force and perspective to con-stitute U.S. Latino expression as we have come to characterize it here. Hijuelos's more recent work, *The Mambo Kings Play Songs of Love*, is a more complexly ambivalent anti-romance, as our white Cuban musi-cians enter the door into U.S. acculturation only

---

[11]Here we follow Nick Kanellos's "Introduction" to *Biographical Dictionary of Hispanic Literature in the United States* (NY: Greenwood Press, 1989), p. xvi.

to lose their lives in machistic assertion, nostalgia and spiritual paralysis. In this work, Hijuelos bears ambivalent witness to a breakthrough toward a critical and oppositional ethnic literature accomplished only slowly in the last two decades and expressed in varying degrees also by only a few writers such as Iván Acosta, Dolores Prida, Roberto Fernández and Elías Miguel Muñoz.

The oldest of the group, Acosta is a gifted playwright whose fine play (and then film) *El Super* is able to capture multiple nuances of the immigration experience, and its effect on family life, friendship, Cuban-Puerto Rican relations and sanity. Another playwright, Prida has now written a sufficient number of plays to establish herself as a talented comic writer able to grasp sex role conflicts and other critical dimensions of Cuban and more broadly U.S. Latino experience. Partaking of the wonderful Cuban talent for exaggerated extravagance, Fernández already has a considerable body of work focusing on absurdities in Miami's Cuban enclave. Significantly, his most recent novel, *Raining Backwards*, is his first written in English. Muñoz's novel *Crazy Love*, reveals his ability to portray several of major aspects of immigration and settlement. His more recent writing reveals him grappling with Chicano themes and their relation to his own Cuban roots in a more generalized Latino experience he is intent on exploring.

While these last Cuban writers and many others seem too assimilationist and conformist, they nevertheless point to an at least partial Cuban entry into U.S. Latino ethnic literature as it expands and develops. In this expansion process, a new Dominican current is clearly emerging in the East; and a few other maturing sons and daughters of parents from varying places in Latin America--for example, Central American writers, following the lead of Nicaraguans Roberto Vargas and Pancho Aguilar in the 1970s; and South American writers like Chilean Marjorie Agosín and Argentine Beatriz Badikian, who have written works which show at least some influence of core U.S. Latino ethnic experience, perhaps interspersed with mainstream U.S. and Latin American nuances.

Finally, there are those non-Latinos whose life experience and capacity of creative projection have enabled them to create valuable examples of what has been dubbed *Chicanesque* literature--including the outrage-creating book by "Danny Santiago" and the much-praised work by John Nichols and Jim Sagel. Such developments are not surprising, as some middle class Latin American children have become subject to the cultural and linguistic confusions, and even the racism, that so many Chicanos and Puerto Ricans face; and as others become "latinized" by their contact with the growing U.S. Latino world.

Even as conditions improve for many U.S. Latinos, others will continue to suffer. The proximity with Mexico, U.S. relations with Puerto Rico and Cuba (even if they change), the economic and political situations which impel immigration--these and other factors guarantee, in the face of amnesty laws and new immigration crack-downs and busts, a continuing human stream into the U.S. and its joining with an even greater population of Latinos being born here already. We can be sure that this vast and varied human pool will be the source and subject of a vast and varied ethnic literary pool in the years to come.

IV. POSTMODERN PERSPECTIVES AND FINAL THOUGHTS

How might we summarize the situation of Latinos as they may see and feel it, what are some final synoptic thoughts we should put forward here to frame our consideration of Latino literary matters? First, of course that there are no Latinos, that the word is a construct bringing together diverse people who while they clearly share certain bases, are often quite distinct and only identify with each other in opposition to the non-latinos and that usually for very specific, contingent and often political, epiphenomenal and ephemeral concerns. This said, what core problems might we articulate that point toward the future--and then, what again about Latino literature as the expression of a non-existent group?

A. *Some Key Perspectives*

In the coming years, U.S. Latinos will be passing through a conflictive and painful process of transformation, marked by constant, contradictory efforts to hold on to their existing cultural patterns and identifications while modifying and transforming them in an effort to maintain relative balance with changes in society at large.

In this period of transition, many Latinos will seek to assimilate fully into capitalist or "Anglo" society, but vast numbers will hardly make the effort. For each person who wants to do so, there will be many others so alienated by a society pervaded by class and racial inequities, that they will not want to integrate themselves--or at least, they are going to experience a conflict between their conscious desire and their subconscious resistance. And even many Latino workers who may want to, will be unable to integrate themselves adequately into the U.S. mainstream, because their marginalized role as cheap labor source will be all too convenient for certain powerful and avid groups in this country.

Thus many Latinos will continue to seek their solace from the wear and tear of social domination and discrimination in what they can salvage of their cultural relations and values.

But Latin American cultural complexes will not be able to remain the same in a changing world; and if U.S. society continues to evolve along its current road, Latino culture may prove less and less able to meet its old needs, of providing all that the governments of domination have not provided. In this circumstance, we can expect to see the possible extenuation of the worst things that are already happening to many people: increased unemployment, increased poverty, increased crime and drug abuse; increased enmity between newly arrived and less recently arrived sectors; increasing hostility among Latinos from different countries; the breakdown of families and whole communities; struggles among Catholics and new Protestant groupings; the survival and aggressive (at times chauvinistic) assertion of only the most negative, superficial and regressive dimensions of culture.

In fact, unless Latinos can develop the most positive dimensions of their cultural legacy in ways that integrate progressive political orientations that are able to win over certain communitarian divisions based sometimes on certain aspects of the culture itself (e.g., nationalism, regionalism, racism, *compadre* relations, *machismo*, *caciquismo*, etc), unless Latinos can form viable alliances and fight effectively for common values and goals, large numbers will be sunk in the backwaters of U.S. life, in a society that will move toward a greater division of rich and poor, haves and have-nots.

A progressive study of U.S. Latino culture involves examining prevalent and potential modes of Latino identification in function of their possible articulation and activation in forging group unity, alliances among diverse Latino groups, other oppressed minorities and class sectors. Identification with popular struggles in Latin America and elsewhere has been a dimension of what is at issue here. The ultimate end is to find bases for generating a viable and organizable political response to conditions of exploitation and exclusion.

While aspects of U.S. development and U.S. Latino culture and history generate growing Latino diversification and disunity (including class, political and now an increasing religious differentiation, etc.); and while certain cultural dimensions (e.g, the orientation toward space, time and death, the way of measuring and evaluating the individual and the communal, the orientation to family and the definition that is given to the family in its extended form, etc.) vitiate efforts to forge broader social unity among Latinos, as well as between them and certain non-Latino groups, there are, nevertheless, other factors, resulting principally from the effects of subjugation, that suggest greater future Latino unity and greater ability to forge at least tactical alliances.

In a progressive study of Latino or any culture, looking for practical alliances, potential openings and points of resistance, etc., distinctions must be made between a group or sub-group's ideology of culture and culture itself--also between the specific cultural products (in art, music, literature, etc.) and Redfield's "little traditions" (or de Certeau's "little tactics" of survival)--i.e., questions of language usage, popular attitudes and opinions, social interaction, etc. We must distinguish between what people say they believe and do and how they actually behave. Thus cultural analysis must relate intellectual and artistic production to more mass concerns and actualities within the groups studied. There must be some determination of the relation between what people say and do, what their leaders and writers say about the people's culture and what their culture itself is.

The matter at hand is one of social, cultural and individual possibilities in a world of limited resources. This question should be confronted at national and international levels as well as in each place where there are concentrations of Latinos. In this regard, the relation of Latino culture and literature to postmodernist currents becomes essential.

B Postmodern Multicultural Crossovers

Clearly there is a problem in applying a concept that is conceived in relation to the cultural state of the hegemonic groups of advanced capitalist consumer societies to the cultural and artistic life of subordinated, marginal and subaltern minority groups. Clearly there is also a correspondence between cultural phenomena identified as postmodernist and the present sensibility and strategies of multinational capitalism which gives some credence to the idea that postmodernism may be a new form of cultural imperialism. But it may also be that Latino culture and literature, as systems within postmodernism, may offer alternative possibilities that can potentially affect and even transform the overall field of relations. This, perspective, suggested by many recent Latino critics, is one that is explored at global and micro levels by Juan Flores and George Yúdice, "Living Borders/Buscando América: Languages of Latino Self Formation," which appears in the former's *Divided Borders* (APP, 1992).

Flores and Yúdice see U.S. Latino culture and literature as significant contributants to the effort to construct a new hegemony with its own cultural practices and discourses. As such, Latino culture and literature constitute more than just peripheral or "minority" modes of symbolic resistance to, but within, a hegemonic system which in effect cancels any genuine potential for agency; given the limits of current oppositional possibilities, Latino practices confront hegemonic norms by creating an alternative if not necessarily adversarial ethos.

The perspective of Flores and Yúdice is best exemplified by the Latino struggle with mainstream culture over language, and the extension of that struggle to other signifying systems. In this regard, they draw on Gloria Anzaldúa's border vision as expressing not just some postmodern indeterminacy, but a new ethos in the making--one which generalizes feminist critique to a series of practices in which "America" is seen as a cultural map with endless living borders. Here our critics invoke their concept of "crossover culture," as symbolic praxis, corresponding at the linguistic level to Bruce-Novoa's view of Latino discourse as a new, "interlingual" construction. Crossover culture does not mean that Latinos seek to "make it" in the general culture; rather it is a vehicle for Latinos to create new, hybrid signifying forms that involve linkages and relations in a variety of often unexplored directions. For example, salsa involves a crossover combination of many musical forms, expresses multiculturalism and crossing borders, moments of alliance, convergence and clash among distinct social groups and sectors. Salsa means creating one's roots from heterogeneous elements rather than going back to some place of origin. The search is not for some original *axis mundi* or fixed essence, but distinct sets of identity possibilities from within the givens of an expanding multicultural universe.

Indeed, a constructivist, transformative view of cultural identity and the overall multicultural context of U.S. life is the central motif in Flores and Yúdice, for multiculturalism implies connectedness with others without any necessary submission to hegemony past or present. Multiculturalism and multi-centrism are not equivalent to some relativist fiction of cultural pluralism. It is in fact their view of identity affirmation derived from postmodernist discourse which separates Flores and Yúdice from Bruce-Novoa's early cultural paradigm and challenges his critique of Puerto Rican culture and literature, pointing to a broader, achieved U.S. Latino identity, forged out of the varying subject positions which divergent Latino groups and sub-groups have experienced in the U.S. Cultural richness is not defined by past myths but the generation of new possibilities, and new, if sometimes chaotic, energies. Latino identity with all its previous characteristics and contours, crosses over in postmodern culture as posing some combination of the most retrograde and progressive possibilities for future patterns of resistance and creativity, posing some of the most dynamic points of convergence and alliance with other, non-Latino groups in a broader field of new oppositions internal to and at least possibly transformative of the entire social system of which they are a part.

C. Literature, the Midwest and Future Developments

With respect to U.S. Latino literature itself, we have to think in complex relations, in continuities and discontinuities, in approaches to and distances from concrete social processes, in the relation between the writer and the group that the writer may be assumed to represent, between a work's hypothetical public or community and the real consumers of the writer's product. Thus, in spite of the Latino population growth and the appearance of many writers and texts, and in spite of the valuable efforts of enterprises like Arte Público Press and Bilingual Review Press to produce and promote Latino literature, it is still true that there are few Latino readers of this literature, except those university students assigned to read a few key works as part of their educational experience.

Ignored or not, subsidized or not, this literature is in the course of developing and deepening; and its writers have been able to express many ideological and material tendencies at work in their communities. While clearly most Latino writers are not much distanced in class background or culture from the community about which they write, it is also partially *because* the writers are not fully typical of Latinos as a whole that they have been able to serve as their community's "organic intellectuals." Thus, more so than other members of their communities, they have been able to probe in the world of creation and imagination certain possible directions of Latino life; they have been able to express but also anticipate certain problems and solutions; they have created valuable modelic constructs which have contributed by positive and negative example to the forging of a potentially better U.S. Latino future.

Given the danger of further Latino subordination in the U.S. and the importance this issue has for Latinos and the nation as a whole, the question of social and literary relations also becomes one of what broader cultural and political horizon the new literature and culture project toward in the U.S. and the relation that horizon may have with Latin America and the world as a whole. We have already pointed this issue through our look at Flores's *Divided Borders*. Before fully exploring all the great questions, however, future studies of Latino society and literature must take some time to consider regional developments as well. In this rethinking, the Latino reality must be decentered from the Southwest and New York to embrace a broader conceptualization which includes the midwest.

Indeed midwest Latinos and midwest Latino literature have been greatly neglected. In the literary sphere, although Tomás Rivera wrote of midwest migration in perhaps the greatest novel of Chicano literature, and although such key Chicano writers as Ana Castillo, Sandra Cisneros and Carlos Morton were raised in Chicago, and finally although there are innumerable writers who come from many other Midwest centers, the overall Midwest Latino literary corpus and its role in anticipating a Latino as opposed to a strictly Chicano or Puerto Rican emergence has been largely underplayed in the national aggregate.

In the process of rectifying the southwest/eastern seaboard centering and midwestern exclusion in U.S. Latino literature, and also in taking into account the newer Latino migrations and cultural mixes, initial premises and paradigms become subject to reconsideration. Thus a focus on the midwest and the new Latino immigrations affecting the overall character of the U.S. Latino population demands a questioning of the literature and mythological constructs involved in the Chicano movement and earlier expressions of U.S. Puerto Rican literature. In this context, most of the symbolic ideological systems emerging out of the struggles of the 60s, are called into question, as being virtually unknown and (here, perhaps the real point) relatively irrelevant to the new populations--even if we conclude that questions of space and time, patterns of acculturation and assimilation, etc., may well remain central to U.S. Latino life and its conceptualization. On the other hand, the recent new wave of U.S. Latino literary production, spurred on by NEA grants to individuals and such entities as Arte Público Press, is so mediated by U.S. literary norms, that the relation of U.S. literary and intellectual production (and the producers) to the newer and future waves of Latino population becomes increasingly problematic.

Writers may very well express the "potential or latent consciousness" of larger social groups; they may constitute themselves as the "organic intellectuals" of subaltern sectors. However they must be ever viewed critically in this guise, and literary production must ever be viewed in relation not only to literary traditions (in the U.S. and in Latin America), but in relation to the everyday life patterns of the larger social mass. Latino writers may draw on their roots to take off, but where do they end up? Will they really be Latino writers in more than name if the older oral traditions and performative/mythic dimensions of their writing fade away?

The vast numbers of immigrants and the initial writers to emerge among them have never read or even heard of Octavio Paz, Carlos Fuentes, José Luis González, etc. (to say nothing of a Borges or a García Márquez); but their culture has been somewhat impacted by these figures or at least by some of the same forces which impacted them. With respect to U.S. Latino literature, we may also note that while most of the more sophisticated contemporary writers are aware of and draw upon the Latin American literary system (an early example was Ron Arias's *Road to Tamazunchale*; more recent ones are the novels of Ana Castillo), others respond more fully to dominant and minority U.S. literary constructs (Richard Wright, earlier forms of Chicano and Native American, but also Jewish, Italian and Irish American literature, etc.). Thus the question remains as to whether, in their growing immersion in a broad literary tradition and in their transcultural crossovers, they are coming to better portray U.S. Latino experience, or if they are beginning to drift from it and coming to express that process of individuation within U.S. culture which has become characteristic of many ethnic minority literatures on the road to dissolution. To choose another, related question: in what ways does the recent feminism of Latino literature anticipate the Latino future or a growing alienation between the writer intelligentsia and a broader, possibly very conservative social mass?

These are matters which only future developments can clarify. But the prediction here is that multiple forms of Latino writing will continue to exist and develop so long as Latinos continue to arrive and constitute distinct groupings; and the further prediction is that this process of U.S. Latino growth, with all its implications for U.S. and world history, will not cease for many years to come.

Here, the final of many points I wish to stress--the fact that many Latinos have recently been proclaiming success for Latinos as a group, speaking about Latino success in this area or that, pointing to the growing list of Latino celebrities. I personally have seen much progress among Latinos. I have known many who have risen to positions of power and respect; I have known many who now have more confidence in the future. And there are many more successful ones than before. We have the enormous growth of a sector of intellectuals, we have a great number of capable people in many sectors of society. Nevertheless, the problems for the great Latino mass continue to be great and even worse than ever. It is not necessary to repeat all the problems, their causes and possible solutions. But we must emphasize problems and not forget them or negate their reality and see the welfare of the successful ones in relation to the situation of the many Latinos whose present and whose future prospects are still not pleasant to contemplate.

On the other hand, to project a less pessimistic note, we should remember that the consciousness of negative possibilities provokes many to seek a more positive future. And aspects of that future may be found in positive cultural dimensions that, often expressed, affirmed and rededicated in literature, have survived the acculturation process and may play a key role in the survival of Latinos and all of us. To say this in another way, what is at stake is the struggle to maintain what is human, human for Latinos, human for all who have paid the price of modernization and who seek their place in the famous new world order. Latinos will have much yet to contribute in the ongoing struggle for a richer human world.

LATINO LITERATURE:
A SELECTED AND ANNOTATED BIBLIOGRAPHY[1]

I. GENERAL LATINO ANTHOLOGIES

Broadsides: Literature of the United States Hispanos. Tempe, AZ: BRP, 1990.
Popular short stories and poems by a wide range of authors. The series has more than thirty titles, including works by Alurista, Ron Arias, Nash Candelaria, *Carlos Morton, Eduardo Rivera, Rosaura Sánchez and many others. (See BRP Catalog).

*Nosotros Anthology. Special Issue of *Revista Chicano-Riqueña*, 5. 1977.
Eight Puerto Rican and two Chicano poets plus several painters and graphic writers from the city in the first Chicago collection to achieve national circulation. Poems mainly produced by *El Taller*, a Puerto Rican cultural group led by David Hernández, the chief poet and unofficial editor of this collection.

The Portable Lower East Side. Vol. 5, no. 1 and 2. *Latin Americans in New York City* (1988).
A special issue of this mainly Puerto Rican journal, with essays and short stories and poetry, as well as a selection of photographs. U.S. Latino writers include Manuel Ramos Otero, Ed Vega and Pedro Pietri.

---

[1] All books that should be listed as "Houston: Arte Público Press" are designated as *APP*; and all those that should be listed as "Bilingual Review Press," whatever the place of publication, are designated as *BRP*. These letters are also used to indicate catalogue quotes. All Illinois-origin or Illinois-based writers are preceded by an asterisk (*). As noted in the "Preface," works not reviewed are marked "NR". Entries written by or with members of the MARCH Research Collective are marked *MRC*. Other direct quotes are acknowledged.

Alarcón, Norma, Cherríe Moraga and *Ana Castillo, eds. *The Sexuality of Latinas*. Bloomington, IN: Third Woman Press, 1991. Repressed sexuality, coming out stories, wrestling matches with Catholic guilt, women on their own, Male-female, female-female relations--in this collection of literary works by well-known Latina writers including *Sandra Cisneros, the editors, etc. (*MRC*--NR).

Alurista and Xilema Rojas-Urista, ed. *Southwest Tales: A Contemporary Collection in Memory of Tomás Rivera*. Colorado Springs, CO: Maize Press, 1986. Twenty-one short stories by Chicanos (including work by Chicanos Alurista, Ponce and Bruce-Novoa) and other latinos (e.g., Cuban Roberto G. Fernández and Puerto Rican Enid Sepulveda).

Anzaldúa, Gloria, ed. *Making Face, Making Soul. Haciendo Caras. Creative and Critical Perspectives by Feminists of Color*. San Francisco: Spinsters/ Aunt Lute Foundation Books, 1990. A followup volume to *This Bridge Called My Back* (see Moraga and Anzaldúa below), perhaps without the shock and revelations of the earlier book, this one presents the "fragmented and interrupted dialogue" of women academics, students, activists and artists struggling against patriarchal discourses, racism, ethnocentrism, homophobia, etc.

Boza, María del Carmen, Beverly Silva and Carmen Valle, eds. *Nosotras: Latina Literature Today*. Binghamton, NY: BRP, 1986. Thirty-five selections in Spanish and English by women from all the major U.S. Latino communities. Sexual and personal oppression, family life, conflicts between tradition and innovative life patterns are among the many themes explored.

Chávez, Denise, ed. *Shattering the Myth: Plays by Latina Women*. APP, 1991. Plays by six Latinas in a breakthrough collection. NR.

*Cumpián, Carlos, ed. *Emergency Tacos: Seven Poets con Picante*. Chicago: March/Abrazo Press, 1989. New edition forthcoming. Seven Chicago poets, including four Chicanos (Sandra Cisneros, Carlos Cortez, Raúl Niño and Cumpián), Chicanoriqueña Margarita López, Argentine Beatriz Badikian and "fellow traveller" Cynthia Gallaher.

Durán, Roberto, ed. *Triple Crown: Chicano, Puerto Rican and Cuban American Poetry.* Tempe, AZ: BRP, 1987.
Three full-length poetry collections by Chicano Roberto Durán, Puerto Rican Judith Ortiz Cofer and Cuban Gustavo Pérez Firmat exhibiting their individual concerns and talents but also differences and similarities related to their respective cultural bases and communities.

Fernández, José B., and Nasario García, ed. *Nuevos Horizontes: Cuentos Chicanos, Puertorriqueños y Cubanos.* Lexington, MA: D.C. Heath, 1982.
An annotated Spanish-language reader for intermediate students wishing to improve their language skills, but can be read for literary pleasure and knowledge. Includes a Spanish/English vocabulary list.

Gómez, Alma, Cherríe Moraga and Mariana Romo-Carmona, eds., *Cuentos: Stories by Latinas.* Binghamton, AZ: BRP, 1983.
A pioneer anthology including thirty stories by women portraying female resistance to spiritual and carnal conquest.

Huerta, Jorge and Nicolás Kanellos, eds. *Nuevos Pasos: Chicano and Puerto Rican Drama.* APP, 1989.
Originally published as *Revista Chicano-Riqueña* 7, 1 (1979), this collection includes three plays by Nuyoricans Algarín and Laviera, Piñero, and Carrero, plus five plays by Chicano writers Arias, Duarte-Clarke, Portillo, *Morton, and Sierra.

Jiménez, Francisco, ed. *Mosaico de la Vida: Prosa Chicana, Cubana y Puertorriqueña.* NY: Harcourt, Brace Jovanovich, 1981.
A reader for intermediate-level Spanish, this book includes prose works reflecting U.S. Latino concerns. Each section starts with a brief introduction preparing the reader for the topics and techniques developed in the literary texts; and the stories are grouped according to general theme. A second table of contents is arranged by ethnic group.

Kanellos, Nicolás, ed. *A Decade of Hispanic Literature: An Anniversary Anthology.* APP, 1982.
A wide-ranging selection from the first ten years of *Revista Chicano-Riqueña.* including stories, poems and essays by Miguel Algarín, Rudy Anaya, Abelardo Delgado, Sergio Elizondo, Rolando Hinojosa,

Miguel Piñero, Tomás Rivera and Evangelina Vigil. Many good things, although the collection suffers from a lack of system and from photo re-prints of varying typesets.

Kanellos, Nicolás, ed. *Short Fiction by Hispanic Writers of the United States*. APP, 1992.
The varied themes, forms and styles of wellknown Chicano, Rican, Cuban-American and other U.S. Latino writers, as well as contextualizing intros. Useful in high school and college classes, this book features Denise Chávez, Judith Ortiz Cofer, Roberta and Roberto Fernández, Lionel García, Rolando Hinojosa, Nicholasa Mohr, Tomás Rivera, Gary Soto, Ed Vega, and Helena María Viramontes. NR.

Kanellos, Nicolás and Luis Davila, eds. *Latino Short Fiction. Revista Chicano-Riqueña*, Año VIII, 1 (Winter, 1980).
Many prize-winning stories by a wide variety of U.S. Latinos and Latin Americans living in the U.S.

Keller, Gary D. and Francisco Jiménez, eds. *Hispanics in the United States: An Anthology of Creative Literature*. 2 vols. Ypsilanti, MI: BRP, 1980 and 1982.
Poetry, fiction and drama organized thematically in one of the early efforts at a comprehensive collection.

Moraga, Cherríe and Anzaldúa, Gloria, ed. *This Bridge Called My Back: Writings by Radical Women of Color*. Watertown, MA: Women's Kitchen Press, 1981.
An ample Latina selection in a book that became a best seller in Women's Studies classes, with a wide range of perspectives spelling out the differences with Anglo-American and also European feminist currents.

Olivares, Julián, ed. *Cuentos hispanos de los Estados Unidos*. APP, 1992.
Roberta and Roberto Fernández, Yanis Gordils, Rolando Hinojosa, Alejandro Morales, Elías Miguel Muñoz, Rosaura Sánchez, Tomás Rivera, Omar Torres, Rima de Vallbona, and many other U.S. Latino writers are included in this comprehensive Spanish-language anthology which includes a glossary and useful introductions. NR.

Osbourne, M. Elizabeth, ed. *On New Ground. Contemporary Hispanic-American Plays*. NY: Theatre Communications Group, 1987.
A collection of six plays written in English by Milcha Sánchez Scott, Lynne Alvarez, María Irene Fornes, José Rivera, John Jesusrun and Eduardo Machado. These plays present major themes of recent Latino experience, focusing on such questions as family, religion, sex roles, and ethnicity.

Silén, Iván, ed. *Los paraguas amarillos. Los poetas latinos en Nueva York*. Hanover, NH: Ediciones del Norte/Binghamton, NY: BRP, 1983.
A major anthology of New York poets, representing Puerto Rican, Cuban, Dominican and other Latin American communities in the metropolitan area. The collection includes many Latin American and Caribbean poets who are mainly middle class poets of exile, rather than of working class immigration. Several elite writers, Jewish writers from Cuba and Peru, and also poems by Puerto Rican prisoner of war Elizam Escobar.

Vigil-Piñon, Evangelina, ed. *Woman of Her Word: Hispanic Women Write*. APP, 1983.
Much good poetry and fiction in this uneven collection of work by leading Latina writers, introduced by Vigil and including critical studies by Tey Diana Rebolledo, etc. Writers include chicanas *Ana Castillo and *Sandra Cisneros, Puerto Ricans Sandra María Esteves and Nicholasa Mohr, and Cubans *Achy Obejas and Eliana Rivero.

II. CHICANO LITERATURE

A. Anthologies of Chicano Literature

1. General Chicano Literature Anthologies

Alurista and Xilema Rojas-Urista. *Literatura fronteriza.* Colorado Springs: Maize Press, 1985.
Short stories, poems and photos in a collection of work by young Mexican and southern California writers, showing similarities, differences and perhaps some fusing of Mexican and Chicano modes.

Cardenas de Dwyer, Carlota, ed. *Chicano Voices.* Boston: Houghton Mifflin, 1975.
Deals with important Chicano social and literary themes, with examples from many key writers grouped to represent different states of the Southwest. A fine introductory collection; Instructor's guide available.

Harth, Dorothy E. and Lewis M. Baldwin, eds. *Voices of Aztlán: Chicano Literature Today.* NY: New American Library, 1974.
Prose, poetry and theater, including extensive excerpts from key early Chicano novels (*Pocho, Chicano, Barrio Boy, The Plum Plum Pickers*), actos by Teatro Campesino, and some of the early classic poems. A very valuable collection, which has never been adequately replaced.

Ludwig, Ed and James Santibañez, eds. *The Chicanos: Mexican American Voices.* Baltimore: Penguin Books, 1971.
Essays, short stories and selections from novels.

*Ortego, Philip D. *We Are Chicanos: An Anthology of Mexican American Literature.* NY: Pocket Books, 1973.
Background history, folklore, poetry, drama, fiction in an early collection which influenced the definition and perception of the literature.

Paley, Julián, ed. *Best New Chicano Literature 1989.* Tempe, AZ: BRP, 1990.
Veterans Francisco X. Alarcón, Lucha Corpi and Juan Felipe Herrera, plus several younger writers.

Paredes, Américo and Raymund Paredes, ed. *Mexican-American Authors*. Boston: Houghton-Mifflin, 1972.
Early collection of prose and poetry, designed as a textbook for beginning students.

Ríos-C., Herminio and Octavio I. Romano-V, eds. *Chicanas en la literatura y el arte*. Berkeley: Quinto Sol Publications, 1973.
A pioneering collection by two important first-wave editors.

Ríos-C., Herminio and Octavio I. Romano-V, eds. *El Espejo/ The Mirror*. Berkeley: CA: Quinto Sol Publications, 1969.
Advertized as the first anthology of Chicano literature, compiled and written by "Chicanos without any obligation to be largely and submissively grateful to Anglo-American foundations and editors." Contains landmark, pioneer movement work.

Romano, Octavio I., ed. *The Grito del Sol Collection-Anthology*. Tonatiuh-Quinto Sol International, 1988.
Major works of the early phase of Chicano Literature from that literature's first major journal.

Salinas, Luis Omar and Lillian Faderman, eds. *From the Barrios: A Chicano Anthology*. NY: Canfield Press, 1973.
Essays, poems, plays, fiction. Two parts reflecting the themes, "My Revolution" and "My House."

Shular, Antonia Cantañeda, Tomás Ybarra-Frausto, and Joseph Sommers, eds. *Literatura Chicana: Texto y Contexto/ Chicano Literature: Text and Context*. Englewood Cliffs, NJ: Prentice-Hall, 1972.
A highly ambitious bilingual collection that presents Chicano writings in relation to a variety of thematic perspectives and in the context of Mexican, Puerto Rican and Latin American literature. Presents a good counter-balance to efforts placing Chicano writing in relation to U.S. ethnic and minority literature, although the editors undoubtedly went too far afield in presenting a Latin American literary/cultural context.

Simmen, Edward. *North of the Río Grande: The Mexican-American Experience in Short Fiction*. NY: Penguin, 1992.
An extension of his collection, *The Chicanos: From Caricature to*

Self-Portrait (NY: New American Library, 1971), with stories by Anglos, including Stephen Crane, Willa Cather, etc., plus many southwest Chicanos, as well as Chicagoans *Sandra Cisneros and *Hugo Martínez Serros. NR.

Tatum, Charles M., ed. *Mexican American Literature.* Orlando, FL: Harcourt, Brace and Jovanovich, 1990.
A largescale anthology including all genres and covering the field. Ideal for high school and freshman classes. NR.

Valdez, Luis and Stan Steiner, eds. *Aztlán: An Anthology of Mexican American Literature.* NY: Knopf, 1972.
A landmark anthology including selections from pre-Colombian Mexico to the late 1960s, with thematic divisions and marked by Valdez's acceptance of the Aztlán mythology as the basis of Chicano culture and literature. Includes many choices that would seem very strange today, but also several classics about *barrio* life, vatos, etc.

Villanueva, Tino, ed. *Chicanos: Antología Historia y Literatura.* México: Fondo de Cultura Económica, 1980.
The first anthology of this literature produced for Mexican consumption, and therefore of special interest to Latin Americans wishing to understand what it's all about.

2. Chicano Oral and Folk Traditions

Briggs, Charles L. and Julián Josué Vigil, eds. *The Lost Gold Mine of Juan Mondragón: A Legend from New Mexico performed by Melaquías Romero.* Tuscon: U. of Arizona Press, 1990.
A bilingual story, heavily annotated and analyzed by the editors. NR.

Cobos, Rubén. *Refranes: Southwestern Spanish Proverbs.* Santa Fe, NM: Museum of New Mexico Press, 1985.
Spanish language proverbs from the U.S. Southwest, with equivalent English language sayings.

García, Juan R. and Igancio García, eds. *Readings in Southwestern Folklore.* Tuscon: U. of Arizona Press, 1989.

A collection of traditional tales, Tejano music, proverbs, riddles, *pachuquismos*, jokes, etc.

Hernández, Guillermo. *Canciones de la Raza: Songs of the Chicano Experience*. Berkeley: El Fuego de Aztlán, 1978.
Bilingual texts of songs as well as music for some of them.

Paredes Américo, ed. *The Folktales of Mexico*. Chicago: U. of Chicago Press, 1970.
Best existing collection of Mexican and Chicano folktales, a valuable background text for understanding contemporary literature.

Paredes, Américo, ed. *A Texas-Mexican Cancionero: Folksongs of the Lower Border*. Urbana: U. of Illinois Press, 1981.
A collection, including text and musical score, of major Texas/Mexican border folksongs and ballads. Paredes traces the evolution of the *corrido* form out of the Spanish *romance*.

Polkinhorn, Alfredo Velasco and Malcolm Lambert. *El Libro del Caló. The Dictionary of Chicano Slang*. Encino, CA: Floricanto Press, 1988.
Very useful especially for those interested in *barrio* centered Chicano writing.

Robb, John Donald. *Hispanic Folk Music of New Mexico and the Southwest: A Self-Portrait of a People*. Norman: U. of Oklahoma Press, 1980.
Nearly 900 pages in length, this volume expands upon the author's earlier work to produce an excellent reference book, including lyrics in Spanish and English, music and discussion of a great number of musical forms: *corridos, canciones, décimas*, religious songs, and instrumental melodies. With valuable appendices.

Sifuentes, Roberto, ed. *Antología del Saber Popular*. Los Angeles: Aztlán, 1971.
Folklore from the U.S. and Mexico: folktales, jests, anecdotes, legends, beliefs, popular medicine, prayers, verses, children's games, lullabies, riddles, proverbs, and customs.

3. Chicano Poetry Anthologies

Aguilar, Ricardo; Armando Armengol and Sergio D. Elizondo. *Palabra Nueva: Poesía Chicana*. El Paso: Dos Pasos Editores, 1985.
Prize-winning Chicano poetry in Spanish, including works by Juan Felipe Herrera, Francisco X. Alarcón, Alicia Gaspar de Alba, Rosaura Sánchez, Nephtalí de León, Sylvia Lizárraga, etc.

Arellano, Anselmo, ed. *Los pobladores nuevomexicanos y su poesía*, 1889-1950. Albuquerque: Pajarito Publications, 1976.
Poetry from newspapers and magazines, providing perspective on, and perhaps representing the beginnings of, modern Chicano poetry.

Binder, Wolfgang, ed. *Contemporary Chicano Poetry*. Erlangen, Germany: Verlag Palm and Enke Erlangan, 1986.
A European collection of 18 Chicano poets and Chicanesque master Jim Sagel, indicating the growing interest in Chicano literature abroad, by a critic who has done much to promote its understanding.

Daydí-Tolson, Santiago, ed. *Five Poets of Aztlán*. Binghamton, NY: BRP, 1985.
Five individual full-length collections in one volume, by Alfonso Rodríguez, Leroy V. Quintana, El Huitlacoche, Alma Villanueva and Carmen Tafolla. Presenting varying moods and thematic concerns, the collection is introduced by the editor and has a valuable bibliography.

Empringham, Toni, ed. *Fiesta in Aztlán: Anthology of Chicano Poetry*. Santa Barbara, CA: Capra Press, 1982.
A bilingual collection grouped in function of *la casa*, *el barrio* and *la lucha*. Many strong poems by a wide variety of poets, including Alurista, José Montoya, Tino Villanueva, Lalo Delgado and Chicago writers *María Saucedo and *Carlos Cumpián.

Gaspar de Alba, Alicia, María Herrera-Sobek and Demetria Martínez. *Three Times a Woman: Chicana Poetry*. Tempe, AZ: BRP, 1991.
Full-length collections by three outstanding Chicana poets. El Paso-born Gaspar de Alba explores in political and sexual borderlines in *Beggar on the Cordoba Bridge*. In *Naked Moon/Luna desnuda*, Herrera-Sobek seeks to revivify past lives and events through a poetry

of memory. In *Turning*, Martínez, presents poems of religious and political commitment that were used as evidence against her in a well-publicized legal case which sought to prove she violated immigration laws by helping two pregnant Salvadoran women cross the border.

4. Chicano Short Fiction Anthologies

Aguilar, Ricardo, Armando Armengol and Oscar Somoza, eds. *Palabra Nueva: Cuentos Chicanos*. El Paso: Texas Western Press, U. of Texas at El Paso, 1984.
Previously unpublished short stories in Spanish by several leading writers (Hinojosa, Corpi, Méndez, etc.) dealing with migrant worker exploitation, encounters with the INS, Chicano generational conflicts, discrimination, etc.

Aguilar, Ricardo, Armando Armengol and Sergio Elizondo. *Palabra Nueva: Cuentos Chicanos, II*. El Paso: Dos Pasos Editores, 1987.
This collection of stories in Spanish includes works by several young and promising writers.

Anaya, Rudolfo A. and Antonio Márquez, eds. *Cuentos Chicanos: A Short Story Anthology*. Albuquerque: U. of New Mexico Press, 1984.
Twenty-one stories showing the growth of Chicano literature over a two-decade period.

*Bruce-Novoa, Juan and José Guillermo Saavedra. *Antología retrospectiva del cuento chicano*. Mexico: Consejo Nacional de Población, 1988.
A very provocative recent collection, marked by Bruce-Novoa's increasing hostility to the ethnic thematics dominating the Chicano literary canon and including several writers (Cecile Piñeda and Judith Ortiz Taylor, as well as Chicagoans *Ana Castillo, *Sandra Cisneros and *Laurence Gonzales) who represent a different orientation. All selections written or translated into Spanish.

Griego y Maestas, José and Rudolfo A. Anaya, eds. *Cuentos: Tales from the Hispanic Southwest*. Santa Fe: The Museum of New Mexico Press, 1980.

The first bilingual anthology of stories from the Chicano villages of the Southwest, based on texts originally collected by Juan B. Rael, adapted in Spanish by Griego y Maestas and retold in English by Anaya.

Sánchez, Rosaura, ed. *Requisa treinta y dos: colección de cuentos.* La Jolla, CA: Chicano Research Pubs., U. of California, San Diego, 1979.
An important collection of stories by the editor, her students and friends, developing perspectives that would be important to emergent Chicana feminism.

Zamora, Bernice, ed. *The Best of Chicano Fiction.* Albuquerque: Pajarito Publications, 1981.
A collection by a major Chicana poet.

5. Chicano Drama Anthologies

Garza, Robert J., ed. *Contemporary Chicano Theatre.* Anthology. Notre Dame, IN: U. of Notre Dame Press, 1976.
Best recent collection. Contains plays by Luis Valdez, Rubén Sierra, Alurista, Ysidro R. Macías, Estela Portillo Trambley, and Garza.

Huerta, Jorge A., ed. *El Teatro de la Esperanza: An Anthology of Chicano Drama.* Goleta, CA: El Teatro de la Esperanza, 1973.
Good early collection of post-Teatro Campesino work. Contains introduction, photos, production notes, brief biographies of playwrights Joey García, Jaime Verdugo, Rodrigo Duarte Clark, Frank Ramírez, Felipe Castro, and Huerta.

Huerta, Jorge, ed. *Necessary Theater. Six Plays about the Chicano Experience.* APP, 1989.
This first anthology of Chicano theater in the past decade presents plays that have met with critical acclaim in professional productions. The collection features two major plays by Teatro de la Esperanza, *Guadalupe* and *La Victima*, plus *The Shrunken Head of Pancho Villa* by Luis Valdez, *Money* by Arthur Girón, *Latina* by Milcha Sánchez Scott with Jeremy Blahnik, and *Soldierboy* by Judith and Severo Pérez. Huerta provides a general introduction and commentaries on works and authors.

B. *Works by Individual Chicano Writers*

1. *Chicano Poetry*

Alarcón, Francisco X. *The Body in Flames*. San Francisco: Chronicle Books, 1990.
A new collection of poems in Spanish and English by a perennial West Coast Chicano writer, whose work carries on the some of the traditions of early Movement poetry. Chronicle will also be publishing his next book, *Snake Poems*, drawing on Nahuatl traditions. (*MRC*--NR).

Alurista. *Floricanto en Aztlán*. Los Angeles: UCLA Chicano Studies Center Publications, 1971.
Alurista's fine volume, one of the "founding" works of early Chicano movement literature, with dimensions of the poet's emergent Aztlán orientation. The poems evoke Aztec myth and world view as they challenge western norms.

Alurista. *Timespace Huracán: Poems 1972-1975*. Albuquerque: Pajarito Publications, 1976.
Mainly in Spanish, these poems record Alurista's confrontation with Mexico and the reaffirmation of the power and influence of Amerindia in his work.

Alurista. *Spik in Glyph?* APP, 1981.
Marking a break with his earlier work, this small collection contains skilled linguistic contortions and strategies, word plays and verbal fireworks, all expressing the complexities of bilingual/ bicultural experience and understanding.

Alurista. *Return: Poems Collected and New*. Ypsilanti, MI: BRP, 1982.
Compares and contrasts Alurista's development over a decade by bringing together his second book, *Nationchild Plumaroja*, (1969-72) and (at time of publication) his most recent volume, *Dawn's Eye*, and tying the two works together with a fine introduction by Gary Keller. More contemplative than *Floricanto*, *Nationchild* continues Alurista's criticism of Anglo domination and affirmation of spiritual vision of the Chicano nation. His poems explore Indian roots while presenting the

birth of *la raza* through new language experiments which yield up fresh words to embody the dualities he discovers. Reflecting the poet's development of new motifs signalled in *Spik in Glyph?*, *Dawn's Eye* (1982) extends Alurista's field of reference to many parts of the world, with a special emphasis on his experiences in Holland.

Anaya, Rudolfo. *The Adventures of Juan Chicaspatas*. APP, 1985.
A mock epic poem in which the myths and history of Mexico and the Southwest are revised in a fantasy dream of Malinche, Cortes and the conquest, of gods, ghosts and *pachucos*.

Argüelles, Iván. *What Are They Doing to My Animal?*. Madison, WI: Ghost Dance Press, 1985.
Chapbook of bilingual surrealist poetry about Latino life, ecology and other movement-related themes (*MRC*--NR).

Baca, Jimmy Santiago. *What's Happening*. Willimantic, CT: Curbstone Press, 1982.
Poems of conflict and identity, with heightened verve and allure, as Baca's lyric power projects his experience of oppression.

Baca, Jimmy Santiago. *Martin & Meditations on the South Valley*. Intro. Denise Levertov. NY: New Directions, 1987.
Two passionate, lyric stories told through poems attempting to recreate the evolution of Chicano Southwest life in the past twenty years. The first story is a portrait of Martin, the young artist as a bad-mouthing but soul-searching marginal mestizo living from hand to mouth, wandering from state to state, gradually drawn to recreate his roots and resuscitate his family's life. But the second story, beginning with Martin's house burning down, shows how barrio types and the whole Southwest world are falling apart, as disintegration and despair, squandered youth and lost hope, drugs and death permeate the landscape (*MRC*).

Baca, Jimmy Santiago. *Black Mesa Poems*. Intro. Denise Levertov. NY: New Directions, 1989.
A loosely interconnected collection rooted in New Mexico and tracing a visionary biography of place. Subjects include family celebrations, domestic pleasures, *barrio* and range experiences, the births and deaths of neighbors and seasons. With a glossary (*MRC*).

Candelaria, Cordelia. *Ojo de la cueva*, ed. Alurista & Xelina. Colorado Springs, CO: Maize Press, 1985.
A collection of poems in which the noted Chicana writer and scholar explores her relationship with her family and her beloved New Mexico.

Cárdenas, Reyes. *I Was Never a Militant Chicano*. Austin: Relámpago, 1986.
The mature work of this Texas poet, with some of his best poetry, mainly in English. Winner of the 1985 Austin Book Award.

*Castillo, Ana. *Women Are Not Roses*. APP, 1984.
Drawing together poems from earlier chapbooks plus several more recent efforts, this collection presents the poet's ethnic, class and gender struggles; it includes several memorable works delineating those social dimensions affecting and transforming desire.

*Castillo, Ana. *My Father Was a Toltec*. Novato, CA: West End Press, 1988.
A collection portraying Castillo's early Chicago years, her relation to mother and womanizing father, her Mexican and Chicago gang roots, ethnic warfare in the schools, and gender warfare in the neighborhoods. A harsh, unsentimental portrayal of *barrio* life, culminating in the vision of another, better country which the poet claims as her own.

Cervantes, Lorna Dee. *Emplumada*. Pittsburgh: Pittsburgh University Press, 1981.
Considered a major work of Chicano poetry, this volume straddles older and newer Chicano orientations. Varied in theme and style, the book has poems which deal with such normative themes like the destruction of neighborhood and home, and the struggle for ethnic survival; but the activism and rhetoric of movement poetry are gone, and the orientation is more personal and introspective.

Cervantes, Lorna Dee. *From the Cables of Genocide: Poems on Love and Hunger*. APP, 1991.
These poems confirm the author's place as one of the most talented Chicana poets on the scene, as they express human as well as ethnic and feminist concerns with humor, power, musicality, grace and complexity.

Chávez, Denise. *Face of an Angel*. APP, 1988.
A sharp first effort in poetry by a writer mainly known for her fiction.

Chávez, Fray Angélico. *Selected Poems with an Apología*. Santa Fe: Press of the Territorian, 1969.
A Chicano Franciscan priest from New Mexico, in his most comprehensive collection of poems expressing a resistance to domination.

*Cisneros, Sandra. *My Wicked, Wicked Ways*. APP, 1987.
Finely wrought poems which project the poet from her Chicago Chicano origins and identity struggles (the world of Esperanza in *The House on Mango Street*), to European adventures, a shattering love affair and (it may be inferred) beyond. Not so wicked as naughty.

Corpi, Lucha. *Palabras de Mediodía: Noon Words*. Trans. Catherine Rodríguez-Nieto, Intro. Juan José Arreola. Berkeley: El Fuego de Aztlán Publications, 1980.
Poems Tomás Ybarra-Frausto has found "luminous and lapidary," and Mexican writer Arreola sees as happy and "full of fortuitous discoveries". Subject of a key study by Marta Sánchez (see VIII).

*Cortez, Carlos. *Crystal-Gazing the Amber Fluid and Other Wobbly Poems*. Intro. Eugene Nelson. Chicago: Charles H. Kerr Publishing Company, 1990.
"Humorous assaults on modern technology and moving celebrations of biodiversity," notes Carlos Cumpián about this selection of the Chicago-based Chicano-anarchist poet's early works, which appeared first in the newspaper of the Industrial Workers of the World (the IWW or Wobblies), have been anthologized in many places, and now finally come together in this volume, along with some of Cortez's fine, post Posada-style woodcuts. Says Cumpián, "All of Cortez's poems exemplify the old IWW slogan, 'Let's make this planet a good place to live.'" Really, the poems represent one of the more unusual expressions of Chicano-U.S. left acculturation, perhaps facilitated by the poet's German and Mexican Wisconsin roots (*MRC*).

Cota-Cárdenas, Margarita. *Marchitas de mayo (Sones pa'l pueblo)*, intro. Elizabeth Ordóñez J. Austin: Relámpago Books, 1989.
The second poetry collection, mainly in Spanish, by this writer from a

farmworker family in California's Imperial Valley who dedicates her book to a renewed Chicano movement. The first section includes poems assessing the movement from the perspective of the mid-1980s. The second section, with poems mainly from 1988, includes broader political perspectives, as well as more subjective themes: questions of love, sex roles, identity, relationships; Latin and Central American culture, etc. (MRC).

*Cumpián, Carlos. *Coyote Sun*. Chicago: MARCH/Abrazo Press, 1990. Second Edition, with Glossary, 1991.
Stressing roots and new directions, rural and urban, folk and modern counter culture, U.S. Latino and mainstream literary trends, Cumpián's poetry draws on Chicago street sounds while expressing commitment to the rural and indigenous strains of Chicano cultural life. Ecological destruction, genocide, empire-building, immigration raids, economic and racial discrimination, Indian mysticism, Mexican defiance, U.S. big city street crimes, Latin American wars, and above all cultural resistance, are subjects of Cumpián's humorous and biting social poems, while others express more intimate personal concerns of a poet who projects a world disrupted by conquest and violation, while he searches for spiritual regeneration. *Aztlán* comes to Chicago.

Delgado, Abelardo. *Chicano: 25 Pieces of a Chicano Mind*. Denver: Barrio Publications, 1969.
Delgado's most famous collection, including "Stupid America" and some other early gems, which established him as a persistent voice in Chicano literature.

Elizondo, Sergio. *Perros y antiperros: Una épica chicana*. Trans. Gustavo Segade. Berkeley: Quinto Sol Pubs., 1972.
Anglo *perros* or dogs versus the Chicano *antiperros*, in a sardonic Spanish-language, thirty-three canto epic of Anglo oppression and injustice. This ambitious work marks an advance in the development of Chicano poetry, perhaps marred for the non-Chicano reader by the ferocity of its diatribe.

Elizondo, Sergio. *Libro Para Batos, Chavalas Chicanas*. Trans. Edmundo García Girón. Berkeley: Editorial Justa, 1977.
The first part deals with the Chicano movement. The rest consists

mainly of love poems to "woman," marking perhaps the difficulties Elizondo and other fine early writers would face in the age of Latino feminism.

Galarza, Ernesto. *Kodachromes in Rhyme*. Notre Dame: U. of Notre Dame Press, 1983.
Personal and social poems by one of the key Chicano pioneers.

*García-Rocha, Rina. *Eluder*. Chicago: Alexander Books, 1980.
Sixteen poems in this first and only book by a promising Chicago poet who published in several journals, worked with MARCH and has since disappeared, *Eluder* traces ethnic, gender and class struggles, refuses assimilation, or female limiting.

González, Ray. *From the Restless Roots*. APP, 1986.
The author's first full-length collection, exploring the Southwest and the psyche. Excellent evocations of regional landscapes related to broad human themes.

González, Ray. *Twilights and Chants*. Golden, CO: James Andrews and Company, Inc., 1987.
Indigenous, Spanish and Anglo-American dimensions (including such modern icons as Whitman, Neruda, James Wright, Barry López, Gallway Kennell and Robert Bly) all placed and transformed by Southwest settings, and subject to transformation in the mestizo, multicultural and transcultural identity of one of the most anthologized of all contemporary Chicano poets (*MRC*).

González, Rodolfo "Corky". *I Am Joaquín/ Yo soy Joaquín: An Epic Poem*. NY: Bantam Books, 1972.
One of the classic early poems of Chicano literature, by one of leaders of the Movement, basis of the famed collage film directed by Luis Valdez, and still a valuable representation of the Spanish/Indian, Anglo/Mexican conflicts out of which the male- centered identity of the early Chicano Movement emerges. The everyman of Mexican/Chicano history, his existence threatened by an Anglo/technocratic order, Joaquín turns to the circle of his *raza*, as he seeks bases for survival in his cultural history.

González-T., César A. *Unwinding the Silence.* Intro. Luis Leal. La Jolla, CA: Lalo Press, 1991.
Personal and philosophical poems, most in English, some in Spanish, some bilingual, by a maturing Chicano poet. NR.

Hernández, Armand. *Police Make House Calls.* Intro. Gary Keller. Tempe, AZ: BRP, 1991.
A veteran cop's laconic meditations about law enforcement and justice: "how punishments precede crimes, how the executioner returns from the gas chamber empty handed, how the cop winks at his partner when he writes up the rape report, how fog surrounds the prison like Camelot. The law enforcer has turned poetic therapist and turned to poetry in an attempt to answer the justice conundrum" (BRP--NR).

Herrera, Juan Felipe. *Exiles of Desire.* APP, 1983.
"The metropolis seen from the raw underside of the seventies and eighties, the metropolises that remained empty and exhausted after the sixties.... The poetry ... speaks to everybody who inhabits the modern city as an exile yet unable to claim the status of exile ... the poet takes over the city, reclaims its myth and horror, turns them into unforgettable images."--Jean Franco (APP).

Hinojosa, Rolando. *Korean Love Songs: From Klail City Death Trip.* Berkeley, CA: Editorial Justa Publications, 1978.
A poetic interlude in the novelistic series. Rafe Buenrostro's Korean War experiences referred to time and again in the novels, told in English language verse.

Hoyos, Angela de. *Selected Poems/ Selecciones.* Trans. Mireya Robles. San Antonio: Dezkalzo Press, 1979.
Intimate and narrative poems, life and death struggles, dominate this bilingual edition of key works by a gifted San Antonio poet. Introduced by Evangelina Vigil, with an afterward by Bernice Zamora.

Hoyos, Angela de. *Woman, Woman.* APP, 1985.
The tension dividing and fusing female and male portrayed in poems that are charged by eros and politics.

*Lazo, William. *The Ching Poems*. Denver. Baculite Publishing Company. Denver, CO: 1990.
A slim, first collection by a Chicago poet now living in Denver. With ethnic touches, and even some poems in Spanish, the collection expresses dimensions of his European military experience, as well as his trips to California, Chicago and his new Denver homebase.

Luera, Yolanda. *Solitaria J.* Intro. Carmen Tafolla. La Jolla, CA: Lalo Press, 1991.
Personal poems in Spanish by a 1975-76 UC Irvine Chicano Literary contest winner.

Medina, Rubén. *Amor de lejos./ Fool's Love.* Trans. Jennifer Sternbach with Robert Jones. APP, 1987.
Love and protest poems--memories, dreams and realities down the highways and in the cities of that country so close to and yet so distant from Mexico.

Méndez, Miguel M. *Los criaderos humanos (épica de los desamparados) y Sahuaros.* Tuscon: Editorial Peregrinos, 1975.
Two mock-epics in one book. In the first the poet meets the *humilladas*, only to find himself. In the second, the poet goes off into the desert of sahuaro cacti seeking his spiritual identity in the land.

Mireles, Oscar. *La segunda generación/ The Second Generation.* Kansasville, WI: Self-published, 1985.
Twenty poems by a popular Wisconsin Chicano, with subjects including sibling rivalry (á la *La Bamba*), untimely death of loved ones, migratory life of fathers, uncles, mothers and aunts in southern Wisconsin, the sexual abuse of an adopted Mexican girl by a white farmer. An ode to Picasso, poems about the brutal news of murder victims--women killed through jealousy, los guerrilleros de El Salvador (*MRC*).

Montalvo, José. *Black Hat Poems.* Austin, TX.: Slough Press, 1987.
Montalvo's third book (the others are *Pensamientos capturados* [San Antonio: self-published, 1977] and *¡A MI QUE!* [San Antonio: Raza Cósmica Press, 1983], continues his effort to portray everyday working class Tejano life and attitudes, struggling against racist stereotypes. This collection, mainly in English, includes an anti-Texas Independence

poem and many others sprinkled with humor, earthiness and many questions wrapped in poems like meat in tortillas (*MRC*).

Mora, Pat. *Chants*. APP, 1985.
Texas desert poetry. Magical, healing incantations that seek to harmonize and fuse what seems to be separate. Traditional life in a world that is at once Anglo and Mexican.

Mora, Pat. *Borders*. APP, 1986.
Mora traces the political, cultural and emotional borders which divide people and give them their contested place in a country and society that is made simultaneously rich and poor by its divisions.

Mora, Pat. *Communion*. APP, 1991.
Tradition and change, female-male, separation from children and homeland, as well as her earlier concerns with Latin American and international perspectives, borders, Southwestern, domestic and subjective spaces, mark this lyrical collection by a maturing poet.

*Niño, Raúl. *Breathing Light*. Chicago: March/Abrazo Press, 1991.
A moving first collection by a very distinct Chicano voice, one more individualist and romantic than virtually all other Chicago Chicano writers. With meditations on Latin linguistic and geographical roots (including a four-part revery over the author's native Monterrey, Mexico and a Malinche poem), the work also bespeaks the author's acculturated literary preoccupations (Rimbaud), as well as a 10-second commuter-subway romance fantasy.

Paredes, Américo. *Between Two Worlds*. APP, 1990.
Poems from the 1930's and 1940's, some published in Texas newspapers and all of historical and aesthetic value, by the famous folklorist, novelist and mentor. The poems reveal a writer whose formal, thematic and overall political concerns mark him as a key precursor of Chicano literature--a role reaffirmed by Ramón Saldívar's *Chicano Narrative*.

Ríos, Alberto. *Whispering to Fool the Wind: Poems*. NY: Sheep Meadow Press, 1982.
Tricks on nature by a writer who shows originality and formal mastery in a series of imagistically strong narrative poems.

Ríos, Alberto. *Five Indiscretions.* NY: Sheep Meadow, 1985.
Prose-poem narratives, often surrealistic and technically accomplished, by a writer who explores the polarities of ethnic and personal identity.

Rivera, Tomás. *The Searchers: Collected Poetry*, ed. Julián Olivares. APP, 1990.
Laconic but emotional poems--twenty-six Rivera published (in *Always and Other Poems* [Sisterdale, TX: 1973] and elsewhere), plus several discovered by the editor in his research--interesting above all for their thematic relation to the author's great and only novel: the search for tradition and liberation, past and affirmative transformation with respect to community and self.

*Rodríguez, Luis. J. *Poems Across the Pavement.* Tía Chucha Press, 1989.
This small collection is a sampler of poems by a socially and artistically committed Chicano poet who reveals Southwest roots as they are re-created and transformed by his extended Chicago residence. Where other writers left Chicago to expand their world elsewhere, this poet reverses the process, bringing border, East L.A. and Watts Chicano images to those of Chicago's multi-Latino realities. Barrio frustrations, women who work away their lives, the lost and the homeless are some of the themes of this collection which closes with a biographical *ars poetica* ("The Calling") explaining how Rodríguez came to write and what he has hoped to do.

*Rodríguez, Luis J. *The Concrete River.* Willimantic, CT: Curbstone Press, 1991.
A larger, richer collection by the author of *Poems Across the Pavement*, this volume details the poet's experiences in Watts and East L.A., as it explores themes of poverty and discrimination, anti-Chicano police brutality, the world of the barrio, the Chicano movement days of the 1960s, and then the world of work and migration, running, moving from family and barrio to the broader U.S. and Latino experience that would be his multiple experience. Some compelling narrative poems and factory poems that seem written as steel is riveted and metal melted. Also poems reflecting Rodríguez's debt to Dylan, as well as Piri, Thomas, not to mention Thomas Stearns E. Only one Chicago poem, but a few New York and Mexican ones. Above all, we leave

this collection with the image of poetry like a tree rising through the cracks in the sidewalk, or perhaps through the concrete river beds of the poet's original L.A. space.

Romero, Leo. *Celso.* APP, 1985.
Poems that make a coherent narrative following the title character (a trickster who tells stories for drinks, and starts to believe his own lies) from birth to the brink of death. Drawing on Latin American magical realism and the mythic qualities to be found in Rudolfo Anaya, the poetry captures life in a New Mexican village so well that Jorge Huerta adopted them for a stage production, *I am Celso.*

Salinas, Luis Omar. *Darkness Under the Trees/ Walking Behind the Spanish.* Berkeley, CA: U. of California, Chicano Studies Library Publications, 1982.
Some of these poems deal with existential problems, some pay homage to the poets of Spain's Civil War.

Salinas, Luis Omar. *The Sadness of Days: Selected and New Poems.* Ed. Gary Soto. APP, 1987.
Drawing on all of Salinas's previous books, this definitive collection reveals Salinas as a major Chicano poet, with dimensions of thoughtful humor and irony, surreal vision and artistic skill.

Salinas, Raúl R. *Un Trip through the Mind Jail y Otras Excursiones.* San Francisco: Pocho-Che, 1980.
The title poem of this volume is one of the classic expressions of 1960s movement poetry, featuring the mind jail or *"pinto"* vision of the *barrio* struggle for survival which was to achieve its ultimate form in Luis Valdez's *Zoot Suit.* Other interesting poems in a collection covering many years of writing that has not received much notice.

Sánchez, Ricardo. *Canto y grito mi liberación: The Liberation of the Chicano Mind.* Garden City, NY: Anchor Books, 1973.
A classic work of Chicano poetry, published first in 1971, two years after Sánchez was released from prison for a second time, this collection presents one of the archetypal Chicano journeys through the "jail mind"--as Sánchez joins his *"pinto"* vision to such key "movement" themes as oppression, exploitation, injustice, marginality and loneliness.

Sánchez, Ricardo. *Hechizo Spells.* Los Angeles: UCLA Chicano Studies Publications, 1976.

Here, the poet is on the streets, but the factory is another prison, as Sánchez explores the misery of the Chicano work world and the need for a "Movement," in over 300 pages of poems and poetic prose passages that attack the "melting pot," and affirm chicano *carnalismo.*

Sánchez, Ricardo. *Selected Poems.* APP, 1986.

A chronological selection of the best work in Sánchez's five previous books, establishing him as one of the "deans of Chicano poetry," one of those who has proclaimed the unity of art and politics while maintaining the aesthetic side of the equation.

Sánchez, Trinidad. *Why Am I So Brown?* Intro. by Ricardo Sánchez. March/Abrazo Press, 1991.

In his fifth book, Detroit's best known Chicano poet presents ninety-four poems celebrating *familia*, ethnic identity and male/female relations. Replete with humor and his wild food analogies, the collection includes many women narrators and protagonists--militant nuns and Central American martyrs, U.S. Latina maquilladora workers, social workers, teachers and cooks; those who affirm and those who reject Chicano culture and people. Lots of English/Spanish, several poems translated from Spanish (*MRC*).

Santana, Francisco. *Tristealegría.* Intro. Tomás Ybarro-Frausto. Tempe, AZ: BRP, 1991.

This book portrays barrio life through myth, oral tradition and bilingual invention to create an intense and personal portrayal of Chicano community life in the process of transformation.

Silva, Beverly. *The Second St. Poems.* Ypsilanti, MI: BRP, 1983.

Introspective, personal poems reflecting on the poet's California Chicana experience. Romantic involvements, maternal feelings, battles with cockroaches and the welfare system, in an identity quest that culminates in an affirmation of survival values and a broader life awakening.

Soto, Gary. *The Elements of San Joaquin.* Pittsburgh: U. of Pittsburgh Press, 1977.

Soto's first book, announcing him as a significant new force: a poet ready to move Chicano writing from rhetoric to style, from orality and performance to literary form, from initial political and communitarian bases to more subjective concerns. The book is divided into three parts, involving urban and rural settings in poems about Fresno, field work and interpersonal relations.

Soto, Gary. *The Tale of Sunlight*. Pittsburgh: U. of Pittsburgh Press, 1978.
In the first part, Soto's protagonist Molina explores his external world and his internal world of emotions, memory and imagination, evoking his real childhood home and a fantasy one on the Orinoco River. The second part continues the effort to affirm Chicano connections with Latin America and García Márquez's magical realism, while the final part portrays Manuel, an impoverished Mexican peasant finding outrageous ways to survive and climb, while praising, finally, the small things in life that are free.

Soto, Gary. *Where Sparrows Work Hard*. Pittsburgh: U. of Pittsburgh Press, 1981.
Contrasts between the poor and the welloff, latinos and anglos. Farmworkers and Ozzie Nelson, vineyard and golf course. The poet returns to his old neighborhood to find it decayed and neglected.

Soto, Gary. *Black Hair*. Pittsburgh: U. of Pittsburgh Press, 1985.
In contrast to Soto's earlier poems, these turn to themes of family, friendship and ethnic identification, as they follow one life from childhood to fatherhood and show the poet rediscovering the world through his relation with his daughter.

Soto, Gary. *Who Will Know Us, New Poems*. San Francisco: Chronicle Books, 1990.
New poems by the Fresno poet who never seems to stop writing slight crafted poems of reminiscence. The cup seems to be running dry.

Tafolla, Carmen. *Curandera*. San Antonio, TX: M & A Editions, 1983.
Poetry by a wellknown Texas writer, presenting *barrio* impressions and images, protesting injustice and prejudice.

Trejo, Ernesto. *Entering a Life*. APP, 1990.
A first collection of passionate, subjective poems dealing with family and childhood in Mexico and adult life in the U.S. "Trejo is a poet of mysteries and incarnations, of secret unnamed presences, of the magical interior spaces of childhood and the luminous floating world that flares and throbs, that burns in time."--Edward Hirsch, cited in APP. NR.

Valdés, Gina. *Comiendo Lumbre/ Eating Fire*. Colorado Springs, CO: Maize, 1986.
Good, effective poems in Spanish and English--an effective portrayal of border history, people and passions.

*Vázquez Cruz, Ernesto. *Esencia volátil*. Intro. by Rogelio Reyes. Chicago: Taller de Estudios Comunitarios. 1990.
A small collection of Spanish-language poems representative of the many Mexican advanced students and professionals who have come to Chicago displaced by the economic and political crises of the 1980s. The poems, showing traces of *corrido* and *norteño* traditions, represent a new resurgence of the first phase of Latino immigrant literature, even as other Chicano writers now experiment with sophisticated, English language new age forms and value constructs (see our Intro., Part II.)

Vigil-Piñon, Evangelina. *Thirty an' Seen a Lot*. APP, 1985.
Winner of the 1983 Columbus Foundation American Book Award, this book portrays the uncertainties, doubts and ambiguities that plagued many people in the 1970s through poetic strategies that pay homage to José Montoya and Américo Paredes as well as through a poetic voice that represents a community savoring its past and projecting the future.

Vigil-Piñon, Evangelina. *The Computer is Down*. APP, 1987.
Humorous, sometimes satirical poems about people seeking to survive, adapting, and sometimes getting lost, in modern urban technocratic life.

Villanueva, Alma. *Mother, May I?*. Pittsburgh: Motheroot, 1978.
A narrative poem tracing this California poet's life in three phases from childhood to maturity. Again stressing birth patterns, Villanueva follows her young self through an often painful and harsh process of awakening, discovery and assertion in which birth pangs and even bowel spasms play their part.

Villanueva, Alma. *Bloodroot.* Austin: Place of Herons, 1977.
A return to the womb, and a rebirth of woman out of the earth and into an enriched humanity--in a prize-winning collection which breaks with poetic traditions and Chicano literary norms as the poet seeks to establish her own space.

Villanueva, Alma. *Life Span.* Austin: Place of Herons Press, 1984.
Asserting feminism over Chicano identity, self over politics, Villanueva continues her work in attempting to link her personal story to universal feminist concerns, and in seeking a realm of freedom beyond the limits posed by others.

Villanueva, Tino. *Hay Otra Voz: Poems (1969-1971).* Staten Island, NY: Editorial Mensaje, 1979.
Everyday life experiences of poor Chicanos, field hands, factory workers, *pachucos*, in a book which generalizes from the poet's personal past to questions of the future of the Chicanos as a people. Sometimes romantic (the *pachuco* is an existential "precursor" of the Chicano movement), Villanueva brings Dylan Thomas and others to the forging of a style that is more richly subjective, intertexual, multi-cultural and "literary" than that of most the wellknown writers.

Villanueva, Tino. *Shaking Off the Dark.* APP, 1984.
A rich brew, this volume reaffirms Villanueva's stature as a writer who survives the early phases of the Movement to write in the upper ranges of Chicano poetry, as he draws on Anglo, Hispanic and specifically Chicano traditions to create his own poetic defense against the forces of silence, disintegration, despair and death.

Villanueva, Tino. *Crónica de mis años peores.* La Jolla, CA: Lalo Press, 1987.
A fine volume of meditative "memory" poems in Spanish by one of the most reflective and sensitive of Chicano poets.

Zamora, Bernice. *Restless Serpents.* Menlo Park, CA: Diseños Literarios, 1976 (bound jointly with José Antonio Burciaga's like-named collection, *Restless Serpents*).
Poetry which vibrates from the tension between pre-Hispanic and male-centered Western culture, between desire and female subordi-

nation, between a fascination with tradition and ritual and a demand for individual freedom and authenticity. Drawing on English as well as Mexican and Chicano literary sources, Zamora creates her own poetic mode in a collection that marks her as a writer of significance.

2. Chicano Novel and Long (Non-Personal) Narrative

Anaya, Rudolfo. *Bless Me, Ultima.* Berkeley: Quinto Sol, 1986.
The most famous and best-selling of all Chicano novels, winner of the 1972 Quinto Sol Award for Chicano literature, and the standard text in countless courses of Chicano and ethnic literature, this book tells the story of the initiation of a young boy, Antonio, through his relationship with Ultima, a wise *curandera* who teaches him about life, nature and death. Criticized by some for an over-romantic and de-realized socio-historical perspective, the book derives its popularity by mixing a *costumbrista* portrayal of rural life with indigenous myths, magic and mystery; it evokes oral traditions and assures their survival even as the conversion of New Mexican life pressures Chicano cultural patterns.

Anaya, Rudolfo. *Heart of Aztlán.* Albuquerque: U. of New Mexico Press, 1988.
Aesthetic problems emerge for Anaya as he subjects his pristine folk vision to the implosion of modern life. Less satisfactory than *Ultima*, this novel presents the story of Adelita and Clemente Chávez, who are forced to move their family from the small town of Guadalupe to a downtown Albuquerque *barrio*. Rural values collide with the urban milieu and begin to disintegrate, as males become chemically dependent, and females become school dropouts and lose their ethnic identity. One son adapts, another joins his mother in fighting to maintain family values. The blind poet Crispín recalls Clemente to those values and urges him to lead his straying people.

Anaya, Rudolfo. *Tortuga.* Albuquerque: U. of New Mexico Press, 1988.
This is a fanciful novel rich in dreams, symbolism and poetry. Written in 1979 and returning somewhat to the world of *Ultima*, *Tortuga* tells of the recovery of a boy who earns the nickname of "Tortuga" or "Turtle" when he is paralyzed and placed in a body cast after a dan-

gerous accident. The novel follows "Tortuga" from sickness to health, as he meets the wise deaf mute Salomón and several crippled children and then falls in love with a nurse's aide, Ismelda, for whom he promises to return as he leaves the hospital.

Anaya, Rudolofo A. *The Legend of La Llorona*. Berkeley: Tonatiuh-Quinto Sol International, 1984.
In this short novel, Anaya transposes the pre-Columbian story of the "Weeping Witch" to a modern historical context, probing the limits of human love and suffering in a world of threatened and fading traditions.

Arias, Ron. *The Road to Tamazunchale*. Tempe, AZ: BRP, 1987; NY: Anchor (Doubleday), 1992.
Don Fausto, an old man approaching death in his Los Angeles *barrio* home, refuses to fade away, but strikes out on a journey through time and space. This imaginative work, nominated for the National Book Award in 1975, was the first Chicano novel to map out identifications with Latin American "magicial realism," and to explore a range of possibilities beyond stylistic variations on an essentially naturalistic tradition. At the most prosaic level, there is Don Fausto's touching relationship with his loving teenage niece. But with this firm ground, Arias projects his hero's quixotic effort to transcend the limits of his poverty and age through the power of creative imagination, as he embarks on adventures that take him beyond the Chicano identification with Mexico to the Inca world of Peru, then back to L.A. for an encounter with a *vato loco*, a group of undocumented workers, and others, as he prepares for the moment of death that has already been redeemed. The BRP edition includes a scholarly introduction by Eliud Martínez and bibliography by Ernestina N. Eger.

Barrio, Raymond. *The Plum Plum Pickers*. Binghamton, NY: BRP, 1984.
Originally published in 1969 during a crucial phase of the United Farmworkers movement, this book became a movement classic, but it is also the first Chicano novel to draw on a variety of narrative techniques even as it presents the ambience of stoop labor and oppression in the fields of California's Santa Clara Valley. The shacks, the robbing company story, the greedy and vicious bosses, the utter drudgery and defeat in the farm labor work cycle are all presented--even

the moment when the mired and exploited workers begin to resist. But protest and the movement toward social action are presented through broadcasts, graffiti, interior monologues, and above all, through a language which finds verbal correlatives for the plight of a people.

Brawley, Ernest. *The Alamo Tree*. NY: Simon and Shuster, 1984.
Probably the best of the San Francisco State U. graduate's three published novels, rarely considered in Chicano literary studies.

Brito, Aristeo. *The Devil in Texas/ El diablo en Texas*. Trans. by David William Foster; Intro. and bib. by Charles Tatum. Tempe, AZ: BRP, 1991; NY: Anchor (Doubleday), 1992.
At last a bilingual edition of this important novel which portrays the Anglo destruction of a Chicano world. The devil crosses back and forth across the Río Grande between the border town of Presidio, Texas and the state of Chihuahua, Mexico, wreaking betrayal, violence and death on the Texas side. Four generations of the Uranga family confront the devil in three historical phases structuring the book. The first part (the 1880s) portrays the resistance of Mexican landholders to the arrival and takeover of Anglo settlers. In the second part (the 1940s), the landowners have become paid fieldworkers and zootsuiters who battle with the Anglos. In the final part, a young Chicano arrives for his father's funeral and decides to stay on to work for a better future. Rich in its language and ambience (involving a mixture of Chicano and standard Spanish, as well as English--matters which make Foster's translation a Herculean task), this novel has been compared to the work of Rulfo and Miguel Méndez for its use of legends, folklore and oral history.

Candelaria, Nash. *Memories of the Alhambra*. Palo Alto: Cíbola Press, 1977.
As his retirement approaches, New Mexican José Rafa disappears without a sign to his wife except a receipt for travellers checks drawn against their retirement savings, a canceled check, and a business card from an East L.A. con man adept at selling bogus genealogies to anxious Chicanos. Candelaria's novel points to the painful sense of outraged identity felt by many New Mexican Chicanos (or *manitos*) and their defensive obsession with establishing noble and European roots, as he follows José's absurd search for Spanish *conquistador* ancestors. Perhaps the masterwork of Candelaria's trilogy.

Candelaria, Nash. *Not By the Sword.* Ypsilanti, MI: BRP, 1982.
Beginning shortly before the Mexican War of 1846, this winner of the 1983 American Book Award shows how the family of Don Francisco Rafa struggles against forces of change in New Mexico and comes to accept and deal with the inevitable collapse of their Mexican world.

Candelaria, Nash. *Inheritance of Strangers.* Binghamton, NY: BRP, 1985.
Beginning in the years after the Mexican War of 1846 and moving toward the date of New Mexican statehood at the end of the century, this third and final novel of Caldelaria's trilogy presents key historical moments in relation to the struggles of the Rafa family against exploitation by ruthless Anglos. José Antonio recounts the events to his grandchildren in a way which mixes successive episodes of brutal oppression with rich and humorous anecdotes which testify to Chicano survival in the face of deep adversity.

Candelaria, Nash. *Leonor Park.* Tempe, AZ: BRP, 1991.
A sequel to Candelaria's Rafa family trilogy, *Leonor Park* portrays the fate of New Mexico lands as they become the subject of family and sexual struggles on the eve of the Great Depression. Drawing on a style that is less "objectivist" and historicist, Candelaria centers his fiction on the fight of a brother and sister over the inheritance of their father's parklands as symptomatic of the greed and bitterness which scars southwest family and political history. The brother's daughter, raised by the sister, becomes the focal point of the struggle; her coming of age signals a new era in New Mexican history.

Casas, Celso A. de. *Pelón Drops Out.* Berkeley, CA: Tonatiuh International, 1979.
A takeoff on the writings of Carlos Castaneda, author of *The Teachings of Don Juan* and other books which greatly influenced Alurista and other movement writers, this book tells the story of Pelón Palomares and his spiritual apprenticeship with two workers.

*Castillo, Ana. *The Mixquiahuala Letters.* Binghamton, NY: BRP, 1986; NY: Anchor (Doubleday), 1992.
An epistolary novel based on letters sent by Teresa, a Chicana, to Alicia, her artist friend, recounting their travels, their struggles for

identity, and their search for freedom in a labyrinth of machistic passions. Teresa's journey back to her Mexican roots dispels many illusions but doesn't resolve her problems; Alicia's efforts to maintain her identity and artistic work in the midst of a love affair ends in the suicide of her lover. A key experiment in Chicana feminist discourse and form by a Chicago writer.

*Castillo, Ana. *Sapogonia. An Anti-Romance in 3/8 Meter*. Tempe, AZ: BRP, 1989.
Castillo's second novel bravely follows a male anti-hero, Máximo, in his travels from the author's mythical quasi-Mayan Latin American world to Spain, Chicago and other points. Máximo's many loves, and his deeply alienated relation with the novel's key female figure, Castillo's alter-ego, Pastora--in a large text that extends the author's range, and promises more for her future work.

Chávez, Denise. *Face of an Angel*. Forthcoming.
A virtual manual of Chicana survival, this novel depicts the life of waitress Soveida Dosamantes, twice married, once divorced and once widowed, and her extended family, the Dosamantes and Lopera Southwest clans; the novel also portrays Soveida's twenty-year relation with her work family, employees of a New Mexico Mexican restaurant. NR.

*Cisneros, Sandra. *The House on Mango Street*. NY: Vintage, 1991.
A captivating, stylistically fine series of vignettes constituting a novel of puberty and discovery in the life of a Chicago Chicana. Dedicated to "*las mujeres*," the book portrays the protagonist Esperanza as she confronts all the negative examples, role models and problems of her neighborhood, dreams of a new home and a different life, and develops the knowledge and language that will enable her to both hold on to and transcend her poverty environment through the imaginative projection of her lived space on the pages of the literary works she will write.

Cano, Daniel. *Pepe Ríos*. APP, 1991.
A Chicano vision of the Mexican Revolution portraying a young man's life torn by the loss of his father in the midst of social upheaval.

Corpi, Lucha. *Delia's Song*. APP, 1988.
Featuring stream-of-consciousness and other narrative techniques, this

is a first novel centered on politics, sexual awakening and feminism as we follow the protagonist Delia in her political work as a young co-ed at a California college in the 1960s.

Corpi, Lucha. *Eulogy for a Brown Angel: A Mystery Novel.* APP, 1992.
Corpi breaks through with her "feminist detective" Gloria Damasco, who solves Chicano civil rights struggle-related murders. NR.

Cota-Cardenas, Margarita. *Puppet: A Chicano Novella.* Austin: Relámpago Books Press, 1985.
"The only Spanish-language novel by a Chicana to date, this is a southwest barrio story of Chicano struggles from the 1960s on into the 1980s. Such pivotal questions as police brutality, women's role changes and U.S. Central American intervention are played out in terms of experimental narrative techniques such as stream of consciousness, flashback, juxtaposition, second person narration, floating dialogue, lines all in caps, press releases, bilingual puns, etc. Using a wide range of barrio voices and linguistic styles (including some vato-style English), the novel invites serious critical attention, as well as the question as to why it has so escaped it." (Manuel de Jesús Hernández).

Delgado, Abelardo. *Letters to Louise.* Berkeley: Tonatiuh-Quinto Sol International, 1982.
A novel about the 1960s "war on poverty" and the contradictions it fermented among many of those who went to work in government agencies. A realistic and personal statement, returning us to many of Delgado's preoccupations as a poet.

Durán, Mike. *Don't Split on My Corner.* APP, 1991.
A new East L.A. novel written by a gang-member turned social worker in his old neighborhood, written with a keen ear for the street-language and values, this book novelizes Durán's experiences as zootsuiting gangmember and reform school inmate. The work probes Chicano gang psychology, the exaggerated preservation of pre-capitalist honor codes as re-functioned in the enclave areas of late capitalism.

Elizondo, Sergio. *Muerte en una estrella.* APP, 1987.
Written by one of the pioneers of Chicano literature in Spanish, this is

a highly playful but ultimately serious social novel using stream-of-consciousness, dramatic form, and other techniques as it tells of two young *tejanos* who enroll in a Job Corps program only to die under the stars, victims of the conditions facing Texas Chicanos.

Elizondo, Sergio D. *Suruma*. El Paso: Dos Pasos Editores, 1991.
Vietnam war vets, Polish immigrants, Mexican fieldworkers, and a young German grandmother are among the culturally-dispossessed characters seeking their place in the U.S. sun--all described by the grandfather narrator of this comic and sardonic Spanish-language novel, Elizondo's second, set in a mythic Southwest town.

Fernández, Roberta. *Intaglio: A Novel in Six Stories*. APP, 1990.
The stories of six remarkable Chicana women in the Río Grande border areas in the early 1900s are weaved into a novel which stresses how the creative qualities of subordinated, tradition-restricted women are channelled into the transformative appropriation and transmission of oral traditions and other dimensions of cultural being.

García, Lionel G. *Leaving Home*. APP, 1985.
The story of an old southern California Chicano and ex-baseball player, Adolfo, as he pursues woman after woman for sex and even love. Set in the final depression years, this novel is replete with comic, sometimes brilliant dialogues portraying the almost ritualistic Chicano process of uprooting and starting again.

García, Lionel G. *A Shroud in the Family*. APP, 1987.
At times earthy, funny, poignant and pathetic, this second novel debunks the Texas past and presents Chicano metropolitan life in Houston as the backdrop for a story of a man who suffers a breakdown because of the social and political problems facing his people.

García, Lionel G. *Hardscrub*. APP, 1989.
Part I of this novel, told through the eyes of an adolescent, portrays the abuse he and his family suffer at the hands of his "white trash" handyman father on the road seeking work and stability in Depression-ravaged Texas. In Part II, the boy has become a middle-aged college English professor who is up for tenure, only to confront his past life once again.

*Gonzales, Laurence. *Jambeaux.* San Diego: Harcourt Brace and Jovanovich, 1979.

The Cajun kings play songs of love or *La Bamba* from the Bayou--as a Midwest Chicano novelist writes a 1970s book about the life and times of a zydeco-cajun-rock and roll band. While Gonzales had actually been part of such a band, he chooses to tell his story without overt Latino inflections, while certainly focused on dimensions of ethnic, bilingual/bicultural experience. His protagonist is a half-Indian who makes a final musical stand with real *hombres* who can fight, screw and dope out with the best of them. Corrupt union officials, mafia gunmen, drug suppliers, sleazy promoters and music industry execs--and of course the available women, the groupies and girlfriends, as our hero seeks musical and sexual paradise, but finally retreats to a rural Michigan estate. Showing writerly skills but no Latino characters, the book suffers from its sexist treatment of women, glorification of drugs, alcohol and violence.

*Gonzales, Laurence. *The Last Deal.* NY: Antheneum, 1981.
Daniel, the U.S.-born son of a Mexican mother and Anglo father, is brought up in Texas by his mother's brother, Beto, only to see his uncle killed by a drug smuggler and come under the wing of his Anglo father, who takes him to Illinois. The story follows Danny's life in Illinois, his early friends and flying lessons, his acculturation and his actual revenge against his uncle's killer who he finds living in Chicago. Ironically, as a student at Northwestern, Danny himself gets involved in drug-smuggling; and it is as a "last deal" in this extracurricular activity that sets him flying back to the land of his Mexican roots.

*Gonzales, Laurence. *El Vago.* NY: Antheneum, 1983.
A modern urban Chicano recaptures the world of his grandparents, taking us to 19th Century Mexico and portraying the struggles of his characters during the Porfiriato, the Revolution and the years thereafter. Finely styled in English and Mexican Spanish, this work sometimes falls into a "Playboyese" that betrays our writer's work experience.

González, Genaro. *Rainbow's End.* APP, 1988.
Three generations of the Cavazos family living in the Lower Rio Grande Valley. The patriarch's illegal swim across the river during the 1930s, the family's migrant labor and Vietnam hardships, their work as

drug smugglers and "coyotes" all emerge in this portrayal of evolving Valley life centered on the post World War II period.

Hinojosa, Rolando. *The Valley*. Ypsilanti, MI: BRP, 1983.
The first novel of Hinojosa's Death Trip series, this loose collection of stories, first published in a bilingual edition in 1973, takes place in Belken County, Hinojosa's South Texas border community, from the Depression years to the 1950s. The manner of the book will be typical of Hinojosa's later works. Divided into four major parts, the text is further divided into smaller pieces, making it a collage of bits and pieces seen from a variety of perspectives, or a mosaic of anecdotes, sketches and vignettes--short *estampas* rooted in the oral traditions of his community. All the *estampas*, however, add up to part of the overall Death Trip story, of how the Anglos, aided by Chicano sellouts, took over the County and began to destroy the very roots expressed in *estampa* form and content.

Hinojosa, Rolando. *Klail City*. APP, 1987.
A new English version of *Klail City y sus alrededores*, which won Cuba's Casa de las Américas prize of 1976, and was published in Rosaura Sánchez's English translation (but with a Spanish title) as *Generaciones y semblanzas* in 1977. The key (and probably best) novel of Hinojosa's Klail City Death Trip Series, this work portrays Hinojosa's alter ego, Rafa Buenrostro, along with Jehu Malacara, Choche Markham, an Anglo politician, and Esteban Echeverría, as they reveal new dimensions of Belken County mores--the injustices committed against the Mexicans, the effects of evangelism, questions of class, the difficult struggle to make something of life.

Hinojosa, Rolando. *Dear Rafe*. APP, 1985.
This translation of *Mi querido Rafa* (APP, 1981), is set in the 1960s and is divided into two parts. The first is a bitter story of Jehú Malacara's job at Klail City's Savings and Loan, as told by Jehú in a series of letters to his friend Rafe Buenrostro. The second part is the work of P. Galindo, and consists of his efforts to investigate why Jehú left the bank to attend the university in Austin. The result is a series of interviews with Valley citizens which reveal Jehú's amorous (and adulterous) encounters and tell us much about life, love, finance and politics in Belken County.

Hinojosa, Rolando. *Rites and Witnesses*. APP, 1982.
Written in English and subtitled "a comedy," this novel presents Jehú and Rafa at a time prior to that depicted in *Dear Rafe*. Divided in two parts, as indicated by the title, the book consists of fifty-one *estampas* (conversations, stories, documents, etc.) which depict how Jehú begins his job as the first Chicano to work at the local bank, and how Rafe returns wounded from the Korean War. Belken County's wealthy Anglo ranchers and their hold on the border area's economy and political life come to the fore.

Hinojosa, Rolando. *Partners in Crime: A Rafe Buenrostro Mystery*. APP, 1985.
Just as Faulkner wrote a minor detective novel *Knight's Gambit*, so Hinojosa concocts his border murder story, departing from his usual manner to write in the clipped style of the popular mystery genre. Back from graduate school, Jehú Malacara is now vice-president of the Klail City First National Bank only to see how multi-national corporations have invaded Belken County and how a crime wave, including three murders, has broken out. Jehú's friend, Rafe Buenrostro, a law school graduate and now a lieutenant of the Belken County Homicide Squad, sets out to deal with a rash of misleading cues and solve the mystery plaguing the town. Meanwhile, Captain Lisandro Gómez Solis from Tamaulipas, Mexico and a number ingenuous disciples come to Rafe's aid, in a story concerned with illusion and reality, as well as the fate of Hinojosa's Yoknapatawpha.

Hinojosa, Rolando. *Claros Varones de Belken/ Fair Gentlemen of Belken County*. Tempe, AZ: BRP, 1986.
This addition to the Klail City Death Trip Series features most of Hinojosa's main characters in a series of stories emphasizing the changes threatening the disintegration of the Belken world. Rafe returns from the war, Jehú becomes a missionary; Echeverría remembers the way things were--in a work perhaps just below Hinojosa's highest level.

Hinojosa, Rolando. *Becky and Her Friends*. APP, 1989.
Highlighting the gentlewomen of Belken, Sammie Joe Perkins, Viola Barragan and others--but above all, upwardly mobile Becky Escobar--as they struggle in a male-centered world, this addition to the Klail City Death Trip series places male-female sexual and power conflicts in rela-

tion to such key Latino concerns as the Church, English versus Spanish, the connections between Latinos and others.

Islas, Arturo. *The Rain God: A Dessert Tale.* Palo Alto, CA: Alexandria Press: 1984.
Divided into six parts and broken time sequences, flashbacks, etc., this symbol-laden work portrays three generations of the Angel family in El Paso, with a focus on the grandson Miguel Chico and on identifications with Mexico in the border region. An experimental and original Chicano novel understudied perhaps for its sexual implications.

Martínez, Eliud. *Voice Haunted Journey.* Tempe, AZ: BRP, 1991.
During a California plane flight, Miguel Velásquez remembers events from his people's and his own personal history. In effect, the novel is the artistic expression of social realities as transposed in the memory and thought of a modern Chicano struggling for cultural survival in the midst of U.S. postmodernity.

Martínez, Max. *Schooland.* APP, 1988.
A child's coming of age and a patriarch moving toward death in a Mexican family struggling with society and nature in rural Texas during the year of the great drought in the 1950s. Rural life and conflicts treated with lyricism and care.

Méndez, Miguel M. *Peregrinos de Aztlán.* Bib. Francisco Lomelí. Tempe, AZ: BRP, 1991; Trans.: *Pilgrims in Aztlán*, forthcoming, BRP.
A Chicano classic set in Tijuana, Mexico and told in Mexican Spanish and *caló*, with discontinuous temporality, stream of consciousness and other modernist techniques portraying the impact of city life on a traditional Mexican consciousness having roots in the Yaqui Indians of northern Mexico. Loreto Maldonado, an old veteran of the Mexican Revolution, now washes cars for tourists on the streets of Tijuana, observing the types who come his way and tell him their stories.

Méndez, Miguel M. *El sueño de Santa María de las Piedras.* Guadalajara, México: U. de Guadalajara, 1986. *The Dream of Santa Maria de las Piedras.* Trans. David W. Foster. Tempe, AZ: BRP, 1991.
A member of the Noragua family goes to the U.S. and meets disillusionment, as old men in the plaza of his Sonora, Mexico desert town

reminisce about the past. Méndez maintains his work as a novelist, once again finding a voice that sustains his narrative and marks it as the property of an entire people.

Morales, Alejandro. *Old Faces and New Wine.* Ed. with revised trans. by Max Martínez, José Monleón, and Alurista, of *Caras viejas y vino nuevo* (available through BRP). San Diego: Maize Press, 1981.
Two teenagers, Mateo, son of a stable family, and Julián, son of an abusive father, discovering life in a Mexican *barrio* during the 1950s and 60s. A disjunctive narrative style replicates the dislocation of values and perceptions portrayed. Mateo sees the decline of Julián's world, his deepening troubles with his father after the death of his mother, his turn to drugs and meaningless death. Other characters and situations intervene before Mateo's own premature death to produce a negative portrait of the *barrio* world. The translation involves a controversial restructuring of the original novel.

Morales, Alejandro. *Death of an Anglo.* Trans. of *La verdad sin voz.* Tempe, AZ: BRP, 1988.
A novel of sophisticated structure and rich ambience, this work presents a complex of characters and situations while featuring the story of Dr. Nagol, a character from *Old Faces*, who changes his name to Logan and becomes head of a medical clinic in a Texas town. An idealist unwilling to grow rich off his patients or accept their racist treatment by the town, he becomes a threat to Anglo power and is killed by an Anglo cop who runs roughshod over the people in the *barrio*.

Morales, Alejandro. *Reto en el paraiso.* Ypsilanti, MI: BRP, 1983.
Presenting the period from 1848 to recent times in California, this book is divided into eight configurations, each made up of smaller divisions which take the reader back and forth in time and language, while telling a variety of stories which constitute a virtual epic of Chicano history. Considered a key Chicano novel for its metaphysical, structural, psychological and historical richness, *Reto* represents a new level of maturity and achievement for the author.

Morales, Alejandro. *The Brick People.* APP, 1988.
Morales' latest novel depicts California Chicano life from 1892 to the late 1940s, focusing on the development of the Simons Brick factory.

Morales notes how the Chicanos forged the foundations of modern California by their labor. His novel presents the effort of a Chicano family to free itself from an overseer and the Anglo family he represents.

Morales, Alejandro *The Rag Doll Plagues*. APP, 1991.
A key effort to bring Latin American magic realism into Chicano fiction. Morales follows a doctor and his descendants as they fight a strange and ubiquitous plague (AIDS?) in colonial Mexico, contemporary California and a twenty-first century dystopia.

Niggli, Josefina. *Mexican Village*. Chapel Hill: U. of North Carolina Press, 1945.
An important early work providing a generational approach to the Mexican immigration experience, cited but rarely analyzed in Chicano literary studies. (See also: Niggli, *Un Pueblo Mexicano. Selections from Mexican Village*. Trans. and ed. Justina Ruíz de Conde [NY: Norton, 1949].)

Ornelas, Berta. *Come Down from the Mound*. Phoenix: Miter Publishing Co., 1975.
An early try at writing a Chicana feminist novel, but a sadly marred affair with little formal interest, this book tells the story of activist Aurora Alba and the effort of her lover, Chuy Santana, a power-hungry city commissioner, to win her over to his political position.

Ortiz Taylor, Sheila. *Spring Forward/Fall Back*. Tallahassee: Naiad Press, 1985.
Along with her novel *Faultline*, (a multi-voiced mosaic published by the same press in 1982), this novel establishes Ortiz as a Chicana writer of importance, overlooked except by Bruce-Novoa because of the lack of overt ethnic reference in her work.

Piñeda, Cecile. *Frieze*. NY: Viking/Penguin, 1986.
Another Bruce-Novoa "find," Piñeda, like Ortiz Taylor, confirms her standing as an important Chicana writer first established, with the appearance of her novel, *Face* (published by the same company in 1985)--again without fanfare among Chicano critics for her "mainstream" approach.

Ponce, Mary Helen. *The Wedding.* APP, 1989.
A comic novel about Chicano workingclass life and culture, including lowriders, *machos* and ruined girls. Told through the eyes of a pregnant bride-to-be, the book uses the presentation of wedding preparations to reveal the system of customs and traditions which hinder and imprison women. The novel has been accused by Alejandro Morales of stereotyping. Form your own opinion.

Portillo-Trambley, Estela. *Trini.* APP, 1986.
A story of discovery and awareness about a Tarahumara woman who, after misfortunes and deceptions, leaves Mexico and crosses the border illegally to give birth to her child and achieve her dream of landownership. Trini becomes financially secure, and decides to return home with her children so that they can experience the relationship with nature she has left behind.

Quintana Ranck, Katherine. *Portrait of Doña Elena.* Berkeley: Tonatiuh-Quinto Sol International, 1983.
A romantic autobiographical novella about Consuelo, offspring of a mixed marriage, who grows up in Minnesota and then returns to New Mexico to find love and pride in her parents' heritage.

Rechy, John. *City of Night.* NY: Grove, 1984.
The first and still the best of Rechy's autobiographical novels, mainly about his life as homosexual adventurer and prostitute, with frequent allusions to his El Paso origins and occasional overt references to his Mexican ethnicity. While the ethnic and homosexual questions have combined to marginalize Rechy from the Chicano canon, still there is legitimate room to wonder about the compulsive repetitions in this writer's early work, perhaps most deliriously exemplified by his novel, *Numbers* and its gay Chicano hero, Johnny Rio, who lives by the statistics of random encounters and orgasms in Griffith Park and other sites. In *City of Night* (1963), the ethnic markings are few enough, but there are some good characterizations (especially that of an aging drag queen) as the hero wanders from El Paso to other cities--perhaps most richly, the glamour-crazed gay world of Los Angeles and Hollywood.

Rechy, John. *This Day's Death.* NY: Grove Press, 1969.
The Chicano protagonist from El Paso runs away from his mother, only

to face legal discrimination for his homosexuality. An allegory of his fate as Chicano writer?

Rechy, John. *The Miraculous Day of Amalia Gómez.* NY: Arcade, Pubs./ Little Brown and Company, 1991.
Rechy surprised with *Marilyn's Daughter* (NY: Carroll & Graf, 1988), a novel about the feminist identity search of the offspring of Monroe and (Robert) Kennedy; now, his ninth novel turns out to be a very good ethnic narrative about a remarkable, revelatory day in the life of a Los Angeles Chicana woman who is manipulated by men and her children, and who must discover and cope with the terrible things in her life.

Ríos, Isabella (Diane López). *Victuum.* Ventura, CA: Diana-Etna, 1976.
A novel about extra-sensory perceptions, a static, plotless work of mood about the development of a Chicana's psyche. Divided into two parts, the book deals first with the protagonist's childhood, and then with some thirty additional years of her life, including her imagined encounters with many beings, especially with Victuum, an extra-terrestrial prince of knowledge. A *bildungsroman--of sorts*, recently given new life through the critique of Ramón Saldívar 1990.

Rivera, Tomás. *...y no se lo tragó la tierra. ...And the Earth Did not Devour Him.* Trans. Evangelina Vigil-Piñon. APP, 1987.
Perhaps the most acclaimed Chicano novel to date, a young migrant farmworker boy's "lost year" of fourteen compelling vignettes interlaced with poetic anecdotes, moments or reflections projecting a hellish vision of a people trapped in a world of chicanery, callousness and domination, but also a world which holds the possibility of redemption--a gradual emancipation from the alien earth and the fears that threaten defeat and destruction. The miseries of the migrant life, the Anglo but also Chicano exploiters and con men, the trip north, the hard work in the fields, the problems at school, the search for selfhood, identification and freedom, all in a small text whose fragmented, fragile indeterminacy has opened up many doors for Chicano/a novelizing. In the originally published Spanish and a good translation.

Rivera, Tomás. *This Migrant Earth.* ed. Rolando Hinojosa. APP, 1987.
Challenging other translations, Rivera's friend Hinojosa recasts the text,

producing an English-language book that is a hybrid of Rivera's style and that of the author of the *Klail City Death Trip* series. Most readers will probably prefer Evangelina Vigil-Piñon's bilingual edition.

Rodríguez, Alfredo. *Estas tierras.* El Paso: Dos Pasos Ed., 1987.
Winner of the 1983 Palabra Nueva prize, this Spanish-language novel presents 19th-century New Mexican people and culture. NR.

Rodríguez, Joe. *Oddsplayer.* APP, 1988.
In Vietnam, several Anglos, Blacks and Latinos join in a conspiracy of revenge against a brutal and racist sergeant. Told through an omniscient narrator and interior monologues of several of the characters, this is one of the first Chicano novels about the Vietnam war.

Romero, Orlando. *Nambé-Year One.* Berkeley: Tonatiuh-International, 1976.
A poetic novel evoking the Chicano cultural world of Northern New Mexico, this book is a direct heir to the Rudolfo Anaya school of writing, involving folklore, dreams and legends as part of a young hero's learning process. Narrated in the first person by the protagonist Mateo Romero, a resident of the town of Nambé, this book features temporal discontinuity and focuses on the ultimately unsuccessful effort of a gypsy woman to seduce Mateo into leaving his land and traditions.

Salas, Floyd. *Tatoo the Wicked Cross.* NY: Grove Press, 1967; Sagaponack, NY: Second Chance Press, 1981.
This first novel portrays how protagonist Aaron D'Aragon, a teenage *pachuco* gang member and prison inmate, is forced to become a murderer or pay the price.

Salas, Floyd. *What Now My Love.* NY: Grove Press, 1970.
A 1960s novel about a teacher involved in the San Francisco drug subculture who flees to Tijuana with some friends after a drugbust shooting and then decides to return and face trial.

Salas, Floyd. *Lay My Body on the Line.* Berkeley: Y'Bird Press, 1978.
Roger León, a paranoid and ex-prisoner who is also a boxer and teacher, survives a series of difficult situations.

Torres-Metzgar, Joseph V. *Below the Summit.* Berkeley: Tonatiuh-Quinto Sol International, 1976.
The sometimes absurd, sometimes visionary story of a religious fanatic and racist married to a Chicana named María in a west Texas town. A college president preaching against "niggers" is matched against a Chicano professor who rails against racism. But the real loser is María, who is murdered by a fundamentalist preacher. Anglo hell and the damnation of all Chicanos who submit in this anomalous Chicano novel.

Valdés, Gina. *There Are No Madmen Here.* San Diego: Maize, 1981.
A novel composed of four interlocked stories of which "María Portillo" is the centerpiece. "Rhythms" tells of Yoli, María's daydreaming, romantic daughter; "Nobody Listens" is the story of María's father living alone in a cheap hotel; the title story is about María's asylum-confined brother. The main story portrays María herself, an abandoned Los Angeles mother who supports her three children with the help of her family on both sides of the border. Family help as a means to freedom, or some combination of Mexican and Anglo values seems to be the thematic core of this novel of a woman's growth.

Vásquez, Richard. *Chicano.* Garden City, NY: Doubleday, 1970.
The first of three novels by this writer is the only one to receive any serious critical consideration by critics of Chicano literature because of its pioneering role. Four generations of the Sandoval family who initially leave revolution-torn Mexico to settle in an L.A. *barrio.* The first scenes are among the most successful of this work, which ultimately centers on the story of María Sandoval and her Anglo boyfriend David Stiver, who attempts to justify his love affair to himself and parents by fantasizing a Spanish ancestry for her. María dies of an illegal abortion he insists she have, and David finds out noble blood indeed flowed from her veins. Thus historical novel collapses into melodrama in a book which suffers from the weaknesses of style, characterization and plot that mark Vásquez's two subsequent novels.

Venegas, Daniel, *Las aventuras de Don Chipote o Cuando los perícos mamen (The Adventures of Don Chipote or When the Parakeets Suckle).* México: Secretaría de Educación Pública. Centro de Estudios Fronterizos del Norte de Mexico: 1984.
A comic, picaresque novel published in Los Angeles in 1928 and then

lost for many years, this book, found and republished by Nicolás Kanellos, has been called one of the first Mexican works in the U.S. to have significant Chicano traits. Don Chipote is a Mexican immigrant worker who travels throughout the Southwest only to return home when his wife finds him and helps him see that the U.S. is no place for a Mexican. Editor of the comic weekly *El Malcriado*, Venegas became a master of *caló*, and used it to great advantage, thereby enhancing his book's role as the great precursor novel. The original Spanish appears with Kanellos's informative introduction.

Villanueva, Alma Luz. *The Ultraviolet Sky*. Tempe, AZ: BRP, 1988.
Feminism made poetry in this novel by a poet. Rosa tries to paint a lilac sky that resists her efforts, as she faces marital breakup, her son's newfound sexuality, the apparent loss of her best friend and an unexpected pregnancy. Rejecting conventional values and roles, trying to assert her life energies and fulfill her vision, Rosa faces the strain in all her relations, but resolves to continue her struggle.

Villarreal, José Antonio. *Pocho*. Garden City, NY: Doubleday, 1959.
Generally recognized as the first key novel of the Chicano renaissance, this is the story of a Mexican family coming to California in the wake of the Revolution, and pursuing a new life in Anglo-occupied territory. The father turns away from his wife, and the wife struggles for an independent life, as the family begins to disintegrate and the son, Richard Rubio, the ultimate protagonist and the *pocho* (or Americanized Mexican) has to seek his own way in life on the eve of World War II. Criticized in its time for assimilationist emphases, for not adequately confronting questions of racism in U.S. society, for its obvious shortcomings of form and style, *Pocho* still stands as a classic Chicano *Bildungsroman*: an early effort to syncretize Mexican and U.S. values and norms, in the search for a creative synthesis.

Villarreal, José Antonio. *The Fifth Horseman*. Garden City, NY: Doubleday, 1974.
An ambitious novel, completed in 1974 and considered a far better literary text than *Pocho*, this is one of the novels of the Mexican Revolution, as well as a historical novel of the U.S. *Peón* Heraclio Inés, a fifth son and skilled horseman, rises in Pancho Villa's army only to betray the principles of the Revolution.

Villarreal, José Antonio. *Clemente Chacón*. Binghamton, NY: BRP, 1984.
A day in the life of man who is both Mexican and American, and whose life story emerges through flashback and dialogue. That story is the rise of Ramón Alvarez, an underclass urchin, from the shantytowns of Ciudad Juárez to the skyscrapers of the U.S. capital, where, taking on his new name of Chacón, he becomes a successful insurance executive who nevertheless feels the confusions and contradictions of his identity.

Villaseñor, Victor *Macho!*. APP, 1991.
First published by Bantam Books in 1973, this novel describes how Michoacán-born Tarascan Indian teenager Roberto García struggles past the border and through California agro-business lands, proving his *machismo*, cheating his fellow workers and *hermanos*, strike-breaking and finally turning criminal in his successful quest for easy riches. Tightly written and with moments of power, Villaseñor's first novel reveals promise but also some limits, as a work which seeks to touch on all the "big themes." The work portrays some of the divisions among the fieldworkers with respect to UFW organizing work in the 60s; it also portrays a return to Mexico in which the protagonist's acculturation experience causes him to reject the machistic code of vengeance which demands he avenge the death of his father.

Villaseñor, Victor. *Jury, The People vs. Juan Corona*. Boston: Little, Brown and Company, 1976.
A study suggesting racism in the trial of convicted serial killer Juan Corona, with moments suggesting novelistic art.

Villaseñor, Victor. *Rain of Gold*. APP, 1991.
This sprawling narrative weaves the separate stories of Lupe Gómez and Salvador Villaseñor as they experience the Revolutionary epoch in Mexico, migrate to the U.S., and then meet, court and marry in California. Filled with a multiplicity of characters, and permeated by the stories and values of Lupe's grandmother Doña Guadalupe, the book portrays *barrio* mores and participation in the bootlegging 1920s--the persistence of old customs, the escape from them into rootlessness, the effort to recapture old sources of being in new circumstances. Hyped as a Latino *Roots* and withdrawn from a major trade publisher who wished to label and market it as a novel, the book is rich if sometimes overblown.

3. Chicano Autobiography

Acosta, Oscar Zeta. *The Autobiography of a Brown Buffalo*. San Francisco: Straight Arrow Books, 1972; NY: Vintage, 1989.
Half novel, half autobiography, this wellknown book describes a brown people struggling to find itself and resist impending extinction. Written by an El Paso born and bred L.A. Chicano attorney, the book tells the story of a big city lawyer who drops out, travels through the Southwest experimenting with drugs and alcohol and finally ends up in Ciudad Juárez, where he begins to explore his Mexican and Chicano heritage.

Acosta, Oscar Zeta. *The Revolt of the Cockroach People*. San Francisco: Straight Arrow Books, 1973; NY: Vintage, 1989.
More famous (and notorious) than *The Autobiography of a Brown Buffalo*, this sequel has our hero lawyer return to L.A., where he begins defending Chicano causes and victims. The book is probably most important because it portrays the volatile period of 1968-70 during the years of great Chicano militancy. Figures modelled on Ronald Reagan, Robert Kennedy, the mayor of Los Angeles and Chicano activists Rubén Salazar and César Chávez are present in the book, which is nevertheless dominated by the author's special amalgam of ethnic pride and opportunism, social optimism and utter cynicism. Acosta becomes Zeta, a modern Zapata defending the Mexican poor who, in the spirit of the times, are seen as the down-trodden cockroaches who need to rise and *caminar*. In the end, our lawyer-hero, just like Acosta himself, disappears from the scene, never to be heard from again.

Baez, Joan. *Daybreak*. NY: Dial Press, 1968.
A well-written book by and about the popular singer identified with the 1960s, this text is especially valuable here for its portrayal of Baez's formative years and her relations with mother and father.

Castaneda, Carlos. *Teachings of Don Juan: A Yaqui Way of Knowledge*. NY: Washington Square Press, 1982.
The first, most representative and most important of Castaneda's books, this volume became a cult text for the 1960s counter culture, but also for a Chicano movement in search for a mythology. Especially influential on the poet Alurista, but also affecting Luis Valdez and many other writers, the volume champions a mystical mode of epistemology

and identity in opposition to instrumental Western norms; its emphasis on drug culture probably mars it as a text for the 1980s and 90s.

Galarza, Ernesto. *Barrio Boy: The Story of a Boy's Acculturation.* Notre Dame, IND: U. of Notre Dame Press, 1971.
A fictionalized autobiography with much of the intertextuality of a novel, this book depicts the life of the author of *Merchants of Labor* from his birth in Jalcoctán, Mexico through his family's escape from the Revolution, and then their settling out in Sacramento, California; the book also constitutes a kind of psycho-history of value for countering the image of Chicanos as a people who have lost their sense of identity in the process of adjusting to the U.S. environment. Galarza's family tries to take root in a new home, only to suffer disaster as father and mother die and the young protagonist has to find work and a means to continue his education. Finding himself in a migrant labor camp, he begins to understand what has happened to his people, attempts to organize workers, loses his job and decides to dedicate himself as a writer who will speak for those still caught in the web of migrant work.

Nelson, Eugene, ed. *Pablo Cruz and the American Dream: The Experiences of an Undocumented Immigrant from Mexico.* Intro. Julián Zamora. Illus. Carlos Cortez. Peregrine Smith, 1975.
Cruz's story, as told to Nelson, recalls his poverty-stricken childhood, his journey by foot and freight train, his encounters with "wetbacks," border guards and smugglers, his experiences in INS and California wino labor camps, his love affair with the sympathetic woman he marries, as well as his decision to become a U.S. citizen and settle down in a small central Californian town (*MRC*).

Pérez, Ramón "Tianguis". *Diary of an Undocumented Worker.* Trans. Dick J. Reavis. APP, 1991.
The author's life in rural central Mexico and then his memorable, "coyote"-helped border crossing, his jobs in Houston, San Antonio, L. A. and Chicago. A clear, often perceptive depiction of U.S. culture and economy. NR.

*Prieto, Jorge. *Harvest of Hope.* South Bend, Indiana: U. of Notre Dame Press. 1989.
The autobiography of a Chicago doctor, his memories of the Mexican

Revolution, his family's flight to the U.S. Southwest, his medical internship in a helplessly poor Michoacán town, and then his decision to work with Chicago's growing Mexican population. In some ways parallel to Ernesto Galarza's *Barrio Boy*, this is the first Chicago Chicano autobiography portraying the narrator's awareness of emergent Chi-cano health and social problems in the city and the nation as a whole. Perhaps most significant in this text is the author's mixture of conservative and "progressive" beliefs and action. A Catholic doctor proud of his Mexican roots, Prieto walks with Notre Dame priests in solidarity with César Chávez. He then takes on his biggest challenge, as the director of a new family service unit as part of Cook County Hospital's outreach into the Chicano and more broadly Latino community.

Quinn, Anthony. *The Original Sin: A Self Portrait*. Boston: Little, Brown, 1972.
Quinn's story of his search for fame and fortune--his birth in Mexico, the movement of his family to East Los Angeles in the 1920s, his struggle for a place in Hollywood. Marked by many insights on questions of anti-Mexican prejudice and discrimination, especially in the film industry, the work also has a psychological and cultural dimension as Quinn probes his sense of guilt and sin over his efforts to transcend his origins and find success and stardom.

Rodríguez, Richard. *A Hunger of Memory: The Education of Richard Rodríguez*. Boston: David Godine, 1982.
The controversial autobiography of a young man's struggle for maturity in a society alien to his background, told to "prove" that the way for Latinos to succeed is by leaving their culture behind them--but perhaps proving that this path, even when leading to career success, leaves one self-inflated, alienated and sometimes constipated. Overtly assimilationist and opposed to bilingual education, Rodríguez was attacked by the Chicano intelligentsia to the degree that his book was praised by the Anglo Establishment for its stylistic qualities and "insightfulness." In making his case, he argues for the importance of transcending the private, familial sphere of Spanish usage to achieve a *public* individuality based on an assimilation process he believes makes possible full success in U.S. society. Rejecting the Chicano socio-political program and standing against many of the achievements of 1960s activism, Rodríguez became the perfect Chicano for the Reagan years. Rosaura Sánchez,

Ramón Saldívar, Lauro Flores and other critics have taken great care to delineate the inner alienation involved in Rodríguez's stance--a not uncommon one in the community, but hardly one available to all.

Rechy, John. *The Sexual Outlaw: A Documentary, Non-Official Account with Commentaries, of Three Days and Nights in the Sexual Underground*. NY: Grove, Weidenfield, 1989.
A re-release of this cult text, which had much to do with Rechy's being snubbed in Chicano literary circles.

Romano, Octavio I. *Geriatric Fu: My First Sixty-Five Years in the United States*. Berkeley: TQS Books, 1991.
The autobiography of the pioneer Chicano editor and U. of California professor--the events and people that shaped his life and helped to shape the Chicano literary movement of the 1960s. NR.

Salas, Floyd. *Buffalo Nickle*. APP, 1992.
A new autobiography by the ex-boxer and novelist tracing his life and his relations with the Chicano underworld of his youth. NR.

4. Chicano Short Fiction, Essays, Multi-Genre Volumes, etc.

Acosta Torres, José. *Cachito Mío*. Berkeley: Quinto Sol Publications, 1973.
In a series of fifteen bilingual vignettes in a style close to the Spanish tradition of simulated transcriptions of oral accounts, a father gives his son simple but wise lessons about life and death, war and play.

Aguilar, Ricardo. *Madreselvas en flor*. Mexico: Universidad Veracruzana, 1987.
A first collection of six short stories in Spanish about Chicano border life, written with austerity and skill.

Alarcón, Justo S. *Chulifeas fronteras*. Albuquerque: Pajarito Publications, 1981.
Border stories of enigmatic behavior and conflict, raised expectations and sometimes satisfactions, by a writer so identified with Chicano Literature that his actual Spanish origins are often forgotten.

Anaya, Rudolfo A. *The Silence of the Llano: Short Stories*. Berkeley: Toniatiuh-Quinto Sol International, 1982.
Ten stories, including three excerpts from his novels, and introductory epigraphs make up this varied collection depicting human problems in diverse contexts and moods. The title story is a rich one about time and nature, portraying a man who closes himself to his daughter and life after the death of his wife, awakening to his repressed feelings of pain and love only after his nature-communing daughter is raped. Other stories deal with young boys growing up in New Mexico, and one even presents an imaginary encounter with the novelist B. Travern.

Anzaldúa, Gloria. *Borderlands/La Frontera: The New Mestiza*. San Francisco: Spinsters Aunt Lute, 1987.
The male-centered myth of Aztlán transformed into postmodern border discourse in this collection of poetry and prose about Anzaldúa's experiences along the Texas-Mexico border caught between two cultures. This book traces pre-Colombian Indian migrations from the Southwest to Central Mexico and then the mestizo migration back north centuries later. An exploration of mythological roots, but also an exploration of the place of the contemporary Chicana and the question of future relations among diverse peoples. (See our Intro., Part IV).

Burciaga, José Antonio. *Weedee Peepo*. Edinburg, TX: Pan American U. Press, 1988.
A bilingual collection of witty essays, among the funniest about Chicano issues by a member of the comedy troupe, Cultural Clash. The Border Patrol, the effort to canonize Junipero Serra, the English-Only Movement, growing up Chicano, etc. in this book whose title is a Chicano version of the U.S. Constitution preamble, *Nosotros, el pueblo* ...

Candelaria, Nash. *The Day the Cisco Kid Shot John Wayne*. Tempe, AZ: BRP, 1988.
Twelve humorous, stories portraying Chicano/Anglo inter-relations and conflicts--growing up "hyphenated American," struggling between old and new values, learning from those who come before you.

Castillo, Rafael. *Distant Journeys*. Tempe, AZ: BRP, 1991.
Vital and original fables about contemporary life presenting corrupt colonels in Latin America, strange happenings in the U.S. Southwest,

and Chicano views of that most un-Mexican Latino city, New York, as Castillo explores the souls of characters battling against cultural dualism, loss, anguish and crisis by their experience of New World norms, imperatives and illusions. A fortune teller tells life's deep secrets for a song; people panic as the Virgin of Guadalupe appears in the most unlikely places; posters of Zapata and Kierkegaard inspire a Chicano dwarf writing his diary about life on the Lower East Side.

*Cisneros, Sandra. *Woman Hollering Creek and Other Stories.* NY: Random House. 1991.
A series of poetic vignettes and stories beginning with some Chicago scenes familiar of *My Wicked, Wicked Ways* and *Mango Street* and then moving into a Chicano Texas haunted by ancient Mexican motifs and taunt and tempted by modernity. Cisneros is intent on exploring and remaking the southwest myths which her Chicago upbringing had left all too distant. *La Llorona* hollers, laughs, gurgles; the great icon of Zapata is deconstructed by feminist construction. In "Little Miracles," Cisneros draws on her newfound traditions to capture the pains and sorrows, longings, wishes and prayers of Texas chicanos.

Chávez, Angelico. *The Short Stories of Fray Angelico Chávez*, ed. Genaro M. Padilla. Albuquerque: U. of New Mexico Press, 1987.
An edition of the New Mexican priest's fiction that brings out his best.

Chávez, Denise. *The Last of the Menu Girls.* APP, 1986.
Interrelated stories bordering on the loose novel structure so common to Chicano literature, as they tell the story of the coming of age of Rocío Esquibel, an adolescent girl from southern New Mexico, who battles with her past experiences and tries out all the available models of womanhood, to find her own identity and place. Carefully detailed and replete with vivid portraits of stock girls, nurses' aides, maids, etc.

Elizondo, Sergio. *Rosa, la flauta.* Berkeley: Editorial Justa Publications, 1980.
Ten short stories in Spanish, nuanced, alternatively fantastic and personal in detail, radiant with local color and ethnic/bicultural angst, in attempting to capture Southwest Chicano culture. A young girl grows up only to leave her love of music behind; boy meets beautiful girl only to find the next day that she has been dead for thirty years.

Garza, José L. *Máscaras, tachachitos, y un montón más. Writing and Art*, ed. Liz Nemeth; intro. Trinidad Sánchez. Roseville, MI: Ridgeway Press, 1989.
A collection of poems, prose pieces, line drawings, photos, etc., portraying the migrant fields near San Antonio to Michigan migrant camps and the Detroit barrio and, from there, oppression, injustice and struggles for democracy in Central America, Africa, and China's Tiananmen Square, exploring the connections of Chicanos and native Americans, and attacks on the term, "Hispanic" *(MRC)*.

Gilb, Dagoberto. *Winners on the Pass Line and Other Stories*. El Paso, TX: Cinco Puntos Press, 1985.
West Texas stories about semi-employed Anglo and Chicano working class males whose marginal jobs seem to provide just enough to keep them in drugging, drinking and womanizing. How they relate to each other, their employers, the women in their lives *(MRC)*.

González, Genaro. *Only Sons*. APP, 1991.
The author of *Rainbow's End* presents seven stories focused on the problems of male chicanos, their father/son relations, their entrapment in machistic imperatives, their role in family crises and breakups.

Keller, Gary. (El Huitlacoche). *Tales of El Huitlacoche*. Colorado Springs: Maize Press, 1984.
A father tries to support his sons through his inventions only to have them stolen and marketed by Anglos; a Chicano college professor spends the night with his son in Disneyland talking about the Golden Carp. This much and more in four humorous, grotesque and cynical stories about Chicanos trying to make it" in the U.S.

Martin, Patricia Preciado. *Days of Plenty, Days of Want*. Tempe, AZ: BRP, 1988.
Well-fashioned short stories by a Tuscon, Arizona native in which progress and modernity run over tradition. "María de las Trenzas" depicts a young woman who breaks with her dull life by cutting off her braids and running away; in "Earth to Earth," landowners buy up and ruin the land a woman has spent her life cultivating; "The Ruins" shows the need for preserving a people's heritage.

Martínez, Al. *Ashes in the Rain: Selected Essays.* Berkeley: TQS Books, 1990.
Sixty essays by a Pulitzer Prize-nominated reporter for the *Los Angeles Times* dealing with the widest range of subject matter.

Martínez, Max. *The Adventures of the Chicano Kid and Other Stories.* APP, 1982.
Literary games in the title story and others, in a first collection rich with examples of the author's characteristic abilities for social satire and literary parody. Dealing mainly with central Texas small town life and with urban struggles in San Antonio and Houston, these stories portray the inter-racial conflicts of embittered communities needing sustenance and even heroes as they face a parched landscape.

Martínez, Max. *A Red Bikini Dream.* APP, 1989.
Four stories and a novella about everyday people (a successful immigrant, a Vietnam vet, a divorcee, a struggling writer) involved in commonplace but ironic, ambiguous and difficult situations.

*Martínez-Serros, Hugo. *The Last Laugh and Other Stories.* APP, 1988
Chicano life on Chicago's southside, before and during World War II, evoking urban cultural pains and finding humorous and often moving ways to portray cultural and linguistic contradictions, the harshness of steel mill-centered life, racism, social stratification, efforts to hold onto and deny roots, the struggle to survive, and at times have the last laugh, in a Catholic Church-dominated workingclass neighborhood.

Méndez M., Miguel. *Cuentos para niños traviesos.* Trans. Eva Price. Berkeley, CA: Editorial Justa Publications, 1979.
A bilingual collection by one of the major Chicano Spanish-language prose stylists, drawn from older Spanish, Indian and Mexican sources, to provide a linkage between contemporary concerns and varied older traditions. The book includes some stories that are adaptations of old border-area folktales and still others that draw on *Calila et Dimna*, an early example of Spanish fiction dating from the mid thirteenth century.

Méndez, M., Miguel. *Tata Casehua y otros cuentos.* Trans. Eva Price. Berkeley, CA: Editorial Justa Publications, 1980.
Original stories published in a variety of places from the 1960s on, and

confirming Méndez's importance as a Chicano writer. Originally appearing in *El Grito* (1968), the title story is a classic about an old Yaqui veteran fighter against Mexican and Anglo American armies who roams the southwest border areas seeking and finally finding someone worthy to receive his tribe's lore and continue the Indian survival struggle.

Méndez, Miguel M. *De la vida y del folclor de la frontera.* Tuscon: U. of Arizona Press, 1986.
Spanish language stories presenting Méndez's previously published and unpublished stories about the border and the people on both sides.

Moraga, Cherríe. *Loving in the War Years.* Boston: South End Press, 1983.
A collage of essays, stories and poems, portraying the issues involved in being Chicana and lesbian in the U.S. Moraga presents sample interactions and reactions, reflections and analyses having to do with race, culture, gender and sexuality. Disturbing in its hatreds and convictions.

Murguía, Alejandro. *Southern Front.* Tempe, AZ: BRP, 1991.
A collection of stories involving a fictional transposition of the experiences of a Chicano who served as an international volunteer in the Sandinista campaign against Nicaragua's Somocista regime.

Navarro, J.L. *Blue Day on Main Street.* Berkeley: Quinto Sol Publications, 1973.
A collection by one of the early masters of Chicano literature, author of the poem, "To a Dead Low Rider," who gives us vivid portraits of the vatos and druggers of the *barrio* world, and the way fellow lowriders conspire to keep each other down. An example, then, of early Chicano social realism, of Chicano problems in urban life.

Ponce, Mary Helen. *Taking Control.* APP, 1987.
Short fiction portraying the domestic, political and economic oppression of U.S. Latinas in a mode that is entertaining and provocative.

Portillo-Trambley, Estela. *Rain of Scorpions and Other Writings.* Berkeley, CA: Tonatiuh International, 1975.
Women as strong protagonists rebelling against traditional roles in this group of short stories, the first major Chicana collection. The stories

evoke key Chicano (male?) topoi (e.g., the promised land) and give them a feminist twist--as in the case of the title story, where a male activist, the Vietnam vet Fito, finds that he cannot lead his people against oppression without the intervention of a powerful woman named Lupe, who becomes his wife only to achieve increasing independence as their struggle moves to a new level.

Ríos, Alberto Alvaro. *The Iguana Killer. Twelve Stories of the Heart.* Lewiston, ID: Blue Moon and Confluence Press, 1984.
Most of the stories in this award-winning first collection deal with children and growing up, by a talented writer with a good eye and ear for description and dialogue, verbal and non-verbal communication, attempting to portray significant moments of Chicano experience.

Rivera, Tomás. *The Harvest.* APP, 1989.
A posthumous volume bringing together the author's short fiction, including "Pete Fonseca," originally part of and then cut from *...y no se lo tragó la tierra*, and two previously unpublished stories, in a volume filled with rich depictions of the dreams and struggles of those Chicanos trapped within the migrant labor cycle. These stories of love, life and death center on the efforts to establish and maintain community; they confirm Rivera's special qualities as a writer.

Rivera, Tomás. *The Complete Works.* Ed. Julián Olivares. APP, 1991.
Including his key work, *...y no se lo tragó la tierra/And the Earth Did Not Devour Him*, this collection, brings together all of Rivera's published stories, poems and essays--as well as many unpublished works. Introduced by Olivares, the book should provide the basis for a full evaluation of a major if unprolific Chicano writer in relation to the development of Latino literature in the postmodern era.

Sánchez, Saúl. *Hay Plesha Lichans tu di Flac.* Berkeley: Editorial Justa Publications, 1977.
The title means: "I pledge allegiance to the Flag." In the first story, a Chicano boy gets punished for not being able to say the pledge; in the final story, Chicano parents receive the flag from the grave of their son who died in Vietnam, but cannot say the pledge. Sandwiched between these two works are others dealing with problems of speaking English and the rigors of migrant labor.

Silva, Beverly. *The Cat and Other Stories.* Tempe, AZ: BRP, 1986.
A collection of short fiction about minority graduate students, small-town and urban California life, mature children and immature adults, cat lovers and haters--indeed many lovers, strivers, happy losers and sad winners.

Soto, Gary. *Living Up the Street.* San Francisco: Strawberry Hill Press, 1986.
Growing up Chicano in Fresno's industrial belt told in a highly expressive poetic prose. Little leagues, parochial and summer school, and church are the core contexts of childhood. Then we enter the world of high school and girl-chasing, the world of Chicano hope, disappointment and determination.

Soto, Gary. *Small Faces.* APP, 1986.
Soto's second volume of prose reminiscences--this one a series of reflections on all forms of human love, on life and death, "Okies" and "Meskins". Told with poetic skill and humor.

Soto, Gary. *Lesser Evils: Ten Quartets.* APP, 1988.
Poetic prose in a collection of finely worked and warmly told autobiographical essays on writing, teaching, women, money, success, love and sex, on adolescent obsessions and realizations, on get-rich and get-laid schemes that sour, on missing socks. Painful and at times angry, the book concludes Soto's trilogy of short prose works with a tone of acceptance, tranquility and happiness.

Ulibarrí, Sabine. *Tierra Amarilla: Stories of New Mexico/ Cuentos de Nuevo México.* Trans. Thelma Campbell Nason. Albuquerque: U. of New Mexico Press, 1971.
Five stories and a novella about life in a small village of northern New Mexico which the author calls *Tierra Amarilla*, (Yellow Earth).

Ulibarrí, Sabine. *Mi abuela fumaba puros y otros cuentos de Tierra Amarilla/ My Grandma Smoked Cigars and Other Stories of Tierra Amarilla.* Berkeley: Tonatiuh-Quinto Sol, 1977.
This second volume on Tierra Amarilla involves witches and witcheries, as it portrays the pioneers of this land--their daily lives and traditions, their beliefs, their moments of joy and crisis.

Ulibarrí, Sabine. *Primeros Encuentros/ First Encounters.* Ypsilanti, MI: BRP, 1982.
The author's third volume about Tierra Amarilla, this bilingual collection presents encounters of area inhabitants with people of a different culture, in ironic and humorous stories about Chicano-Anglo conflicts.

Ulibarrí, Sabine. *The Condor and Other Stories /El Condor y otros cuentos.* APP, 1988.
These stories include ones set in Ecuador and other parts of South America, as well as in the U.S. southwest. Above all, the stories depict Chicano cultural conflicts in the evolution of modern New Mexico.

Ulibarrí, Sabine. *El gobernador Glu Glu y otros cuentos/ Governor Glu Glu and Other Stories.* Tempe, AZ: BRP, 1988.
This collection continues the author's presentation of Southwest Chicano customs and mores, as he projects commonplace characters into remarkable and whimsical circumstances. First, we encounter Mamá Guantes, a woman with black gloves, who harbors a dark secret; then the "pioneer rabbit," a figure of allegory who has all the best qualities--and, finally, the Governor himself, who overcomes all, including himself, to rise to unforseen heights, glory and fortune.

Ulica, Jorge (Julio G. Arce). *Crónicas diabólicas*, compiled by Juan Rodríguez. Boulder, CO: Maize Press, 1982.
Satirical social commentaries in which "Jorge Ulica", a first-generation Mexican, captures the false pretenses of middle-class Mexicans (pochos) living in the U.S. during the 1920's.

Viramontes, Helena María. *The Moths and Other Stories.* APP, 1985.
Eight stories exploring feminine roles and expectations, portraying the impact of repression on women and the price paid by those who attempt to challenge these conditions. A tomboy's relation with her grandmother; a widowed housewife musing about her years of domestic enclosure. These richly imagined and finely drawn stories make use of interior monologue, nonlinear time, and other techniques, as Viramontes writes of the female body and creativity, of family as source of strength and problem, as she traces women's lives from childhood to old age.

5. Chicano Drama

Avedaño, Fausto. *El corrido de California: A Three Act Play*. Berkeley: Editorial Justa, 1979.
A Mexican mayor tries to remain neutral, while his son resists the U.S. invasion of California in 1846, in a bilingual historical drama which ends with John C. Calhoun urging fellow senators to abandon their stances on Manifest Destiny and California annexation.

Hernández, Alfonso. *The False Advent of Mary's Child and Other Plays*. Berkeley: Editorial Justa, 1979.
The title play presents a suspenseful weave of witchcraft in relation to themes of religion, sexuality and purity; *Every Family Has One* portrays class exploitation; *The Imperfect Bachelor* satirizes consumer society.

León, Nephtalí de. *Five Plays*. Denver: Totinem Publications, 1972.
Emulating *Teatro Campesino*'s early *actos*, these plays depict Chicano social problems. *The Death of Ernesto Nerios* portrays the police shooting of a young Lubbock, Texas Chicano; *Chicanos! The Living and the Dead* presents Che Guevara and Rubén Salazar, (the Chicano journalist killed in the 1970 L.A. Chicano moratorium), speaking on behalf of the oppressed in a play mainly focused on Chicano problems in the school system; *Play Number 9* equates Chicano oppression with the situation of *Prometheus Bound*; *The Judging Man Shows Death* and other allegorical figures arguing over their claims on Humankind after the earth has been levelled by war; *The Flies* comically portrays Chicanos as flies who can be as cruel as any one else.

Moraga, Cherríe. *Giving Up the Ghost*. Novato, CA: West End Press, 1986.
Premiered as a staged reading by the Foot of the Mountain Theatre of Minneapolis in June of 1984, this play is one of the first ones to treat Chicano ethnic and sexual questions from an overtly lesbian feminist perspective which some have mistakenly claimed marks a new direction in Chicano literature (just see Estela Portillo Trambley's *The Day of the Swallows* [1971] where a lesbian, much abused by men, mutilates a young man who has witnessed her affair with an ex-prostitute). While perhaps richer in sexual than in ethnic terms, Moraga's play is im-

portant also for its literary qualities, which have been praised by Tomás Ybarro-Frausto and other top Chicano critics.

*Morton, Carlos. *The Many Deaths of Danny Rosales and Other Plays*. APP, 1983.
The first collection by the Chicago born playwright whose plays are among the most widely produced of any Chicano writer. Moving from agit-prop and social drama to broadly conceived history plays and comedies, Morton's work crosses and combines many genres as he seeks new modes to express dimensions of Chicano experience. The title play portrays a situation of racial injustice told through flashbacks, as an Anglo police chief is tried and virtually exonerated for his premeditated shotgun killing of a Chicano. As for the other plays, *Rancho Hollywood* is a farcical history of the Californianos spoofing the stereotypical presentations of Latinos on TV; *El Jardín* is a takeoff on the Garden of Eden story which probes the Chicano land-centered mythology; *Los Dorados*, perhaps the weakest of the works, is another farcical history--this time covering a century and a half in "a mixture of fact and fiction about the clash between Native Americans and Spanish Conquistadors in Southern California" (Morton).

*Morton, Carlos. *Johnny Tenorio and Other Plays*, APP 1991.
New playful, sometimes diabolical and didactic comedies, including Chicano versions of Moliere's Don Juan and Miser plays, "Johnny Tenorio" (1983) and "The Miser of México" (1989), as well as his devilish "Pancho Diablo" (1987) and savory "Savior" (1986).

Portillo-Trambley, Estela. *Sor Juana and Other Plays*. Ypsilanti, MI: BRP, 1983.
Four plays by a Chicana playwright whose work shows assertive women attempting to act against and yet also draw from Anglo imperatives and Mexican customs. The title play is a historical work portraying an episode from the life of the famous nun and feminist writer of colonial Mexico. *Blacklight* depicts the disintegration of a Mexican border town family, in an experimental mode which combines a story of undocumented workers with appearances of Aztec gods. Other plays include *Puente Negro* and *Autumn Gold*.

Valdez, Luis y el Teatro Campesino. *Actos and Pensamiento Serpentino*. APP, 1989.
Several of the classic Teatro Campesino one-act plays, or *actos* (including *Las Dos Caras del Patroncito, La Quinta Temporada, Los Vendidos, No Saco Nada de la Escuela, The Militants, Huelguistas, Vietnam Campesino* and *Soldado Razo*), along with an introductory essay and a long philosophical poem based on Valdez's Chicano version of Mayan thought and cosmology presenting a historical-mythological framework for the more recent plays and other manifestations of emergent Chicano culture.

Valdez, Luis. *Zoot Suit and Other Plays*. APP, 1992.
Introduced by Jorge Huerta, this collection features Valdez's classic play (and latter movie) about L.A. *pachucos*, their attitudes and conflicts, as they clash with their parents, rival groups, the military, the general public and themselves, and are subjected to brutal apprehension, arrest, and then unfair treatment in the courts and prisons. Based on the famous Sleepy Hollow Lagoon case of 1943, the play combines the author's early theatrical modes of social portrayal with his later mythical emphases, to generate a striking work of stylized theatricality. Criticized for Valdez's effort to link *pachuco* defiance and alienation to the beginnings of the Chicano movement, the work is noteworthy for its zig-zag narrative line and musicalized form, for its combination of pre-Colombian motifs with 1940s stylization, the classic Spanish conceit of the world as theater joined with the Chicano movement identification of the world as jail. Most impressive in the film version (finally available on video) are the Pachuca Andrews sisters and, above all, the mythical *pachuco* portrayed by a young J. Edward Olmos.

III. U.S. PUERTO RICAN LITERATURE

A. Anthologies of U.S. Puerto Rican Literature

Alegría, Ricardo E., ed. *The Three Wishes: A Collection of Puerto Rican Folktales*. NY: Harcourt, Brace and World, Inc. 1969.
A useful collection providing some of the sources of Puerto Rican imaginative projection.

Algarín, Miguel and Miguel Piñero, ed. *Nuyorican Poetry: An Anthology of Puerto Rican Words and Feelings*. NY: William Morrow, 1975.
Based on two years of experimentation on the Lower East Side, this is the first fullscale collection of New York Puerto Rican poetry by self-defined Nuyoricans. Algarín's introductions serve as a manifesto to a selection divided according to stylistic and ideological characteristics. Starting with everyday speech, which he shows to be poetic, he goes on to classify the poets' work according to a continuum of stages in Nuyorican writing: "outlaw," "evolutionary" and "dusmic" poetry (see Introductory essay).

Antush, John, ed. *Recent Puerto Rican Theater: Five Plays from New York*. APP, 1991.
Contemporary plays in English including "Bodega" by Federico Fraguada, "Family Scenes" by Ivette M. Ramírez, "Midnight Blues" by Juan Shamsul Alam, "Ariano" by Richard V. Izrizarry and "First Class" by Candido Tirado. NR.

Babín, Maria Teresa and Stan Steiner, eds. *Borinquen: An Anthology of Puerto Rican Literature*. NY: Vintage, 1974.
Focused mainly on Island writers and only according some attention to U.S.-based Puerto Rican writers toward the end, this anthology was designed to parallel Steiner's work with Luis Valdez on *Aztlán*. U.S. writers appearing include Piri Thomas, Victor Hernández Cruz, Pedro Pietri, Jack Agüeros, Luis Quero Chiesa, Migdalia Rivera and *Edwin Claudio. There is also a selection from David García's "Mass of the People," which sets forth Lower East Side New York political and religious concerns.

*Barradas, Efraín and Rafael Rodríguez, eds. *Herejes y mitificadores: Muestra de poesía puertorriqueña en los Estados Unidos*. Río Piedras: Huracán, 1981.
A collection of U.S. Puerto Rican and Nuyorican poetry, marred by blank spaces for poems not translated. In his fine introduction Barradas notes the mutual ignorance of island and New York poets and the tendency of the latter toward mythmaking and/or demythifying, heretical constructs with respect to Puerto Rican culture and identity. Spanish language introduction, but bilingual selection when possible.

López-Adorno, Pedro. *Papiros de Babel: Antología de la poesía puertorriqueña en Nueva York*. Río Piedras, PR: Editorial de la Universidad de Puerto Rico, 1991.
With a general introduction, bio-bibliographical sketches and a valuable "Selected Bibliography" by the editor, a professor at Hunter College, this Spanish-language volume (including the English versions of those poems initially written in that language) is a valuable compendium taking us back before Julia de Burgos and on through recent writers, including such recent figures as Elizam Escobar, Giannina Braschi and Martín Espada. The selection does not attempt any division between the transplanted middle sector poetry of Iris Zavala, Iván Silén, etc. and the more ethnic, street poetry we identify with the Nuyorican writers of the 1970s; unfortunately its New York focus leaves out Illinois writers like David Hernández and Carmen Pursifull (but Pursifull is as "New York" as the Boston-based Espada). Surprisingly, such early figures as Meléndez and such key contemporary writers as Ortiz Cofer and Hernández-Cruz are excluded. These caveats aside, this is undoubtedly a major anthology, involving several writers undiscussed by other commentators of U.S. Puerto Rican literature.

Marzán, Julio. *Inventing a Word: An Anthology of Twentieth Century Puerto Rican Poetry*. NY: Columbia U. Press, 1980.
Island and New York poetry in a bilingual anthology featuring most of the major writers up to the year of publication.

Matilla, Alfredo and Iván Silén, eds. *The Puerto Rican Poets*. NY: Bantam, 1972.
A mixture of well-known Island and young Nuyorican writers, in the first bilingual anthology to cover the full scope of twentieth century

Puerto Rican poetry. The authors tend to emphasize exile poetry which they find to be similar in style and subject matter to poetry found on the island. All recent Puerto Rican poetry responds to negative social and cultural circumstances found in Puerto Rico and New York; the poets resist as they seek to maintain their ties to a viable community.

Reyes Rivera, Louis, ed. *Poets in Motion.* NY: Shamal, 1976.
Black and Puerto Rican poetry, including work by the editor.

Reyes Rivera, Louis, ed. *Women Arise.* NY: Shamal, 1978.
Poetry by many minority women writers, including Sandra M. Esteves.

Turner, Faythe, ed. *Puerto Rican Writers at Home in the USA.* Seattle, WA: Open Hand Publishing Company, 1991.
A state-of-the-art anthology of prose and poetry, including work by most of the Nuyorican (but not Illinois Rican) writers presented below.

B. Works by Individual U.S. Puerto Rican Writers

1. U.S. Puerto Rican Poetry

Algarín, Miguel. *Mongo Affair.* NY: Nuyorican, 1978.
A trip in search of freedom through the Nuyorican Poets' Cafe to various places in the U.S. and Europe. In his first volume of poetry, Algarín assets that Puerto Ricans are poetic by nature, but muffled by U.S. domination. He seeks to replicate and reveal the essence of true Nuyorican speech. Accessible and performative in style, the poems are marked by code-switching underscored by repeated rhythm patterns which Algarín considers central to Nuyorican talking style.

Algarín, Miguel. *On Call.* APP, 1980.
Street people, musicians, dancers and poets from New York and San Francisco join in an aesthetic celebration and exploration of roots.

Algarín, Miguel. *Body Bee Calling from the 21st Century.* APP, 1982.
The poet takes risks in sexuality as he embarks on a bionic journey through his own body in a search for transcendent experience and love.

Algarín, Miguel. *Time's Now/ Ya es tiempo.* APP, 1985
Winner of the 1985 Before Columbus Foundation American Book Award, this text is a direct combination of interior and street experiences that transport the writer to Central America and other fields of action on his way to spiritual breakthrough.

Escobar, Elizam. *Discurso a la noche y Sonia Semenovna.* San Juan: Quimera Editores, 1985.
Poems by the brilliant Independentista painter and polemicist imprisoned since 1980 for his political activity.

Espada, Martín. *The Immigrant Iceboy's Bolero.* NY: Waterfront, 1987.
Originally published by Editorial Cordillera in 1982, this first book by a Brooklyn-born Puerto Rican lawyer and poet living in Boston shows his capacity for creative transformations. Illustrated with photos by the poet's photographer father, Frank.

Espada, Martín. *Trumpets from the Islands of Their Eviction.* Tempe, AZ: BRP, 1988.
Poetic portraits depicting the personal eviction--the unfulfilled dreams, the insanity, the drinking, pesticide poisonings, Vietnam wounds, firing squads, and other ways of dying, as well as overall questions of language and identity-- common to thousands of Puerto Ricans, who, starting with Operation Bootstrap in the 1950s, were encouraged and pressured to leave for the U.S. With a forward by poet Robert Creeley, and a 21-page introduction by Diana Vélez including backgrounds about the Rican and personal contexts affecting Espada's work (*MRC*).

Espada, Martín. *Rebellion is the Circle of a Lover's Hands. Rebelión es el giro de manos del amante.* Spanish trans. by Camilo Pérez Bustillo. Willimantic, CT: Curbstone Press, 1990.
This third collection by Espada mainly portrays the tradition of resistance and rebellion rooted in the Independentista movement of the 1930s and extending to contemporary East Coast struggles. Hands appear in poem after poem, marking continuities and connections among countless strands of U.S. Rican life and the many concerns of the advocate lawyer-poet, as he generalizes beyond his own people's problems to those of Nicaraguans, Chicano farmworkers and others put

upon by the powers that be. Above all, this is a book of victories in the face of countless reasons for defeat (with *MRC*).

Esteves, Sandra María. *Yerba Buena*. NY: Greenfield Review, 1982. Definition and affirmation as an urban, U.S. Puerto Rican (colonized but struggling) woman are the themes in this first collection of rythmic, driven poems by the most wellknown Nuyorican woman poet.

Esteves, Sandra María. *Bluestown Mockingbird Mambo*. APP, 1990. Afro-Cuban fusions with spirituals, blues and jazz as transposed into Puerto Rican feminist critique and poetic aestheticism, in the writer's new collection. NR.

Figueroa, José Angel. *Noo Jork*. trans. Victor Fernández Fragoso. San Juan: Instituto de Cultura Puertorriqueña, 1981.
Probably the most accomplished volume by one of the most anthologized Nuyorican street poets of the 1970s. The author's surrealist bent becomes more marked here than in his earlier (and publisher-bowdlerized) volume, *East 110th Street* (Detroit: Broadside, 1973), as he projects craziness, chaos, romanticism and sometime humor as an expression of Nuyorican experience.

*Hernández, David. *Roof Top Piper*. Chicago: Tía Chucha Press, 1991. At last an attractive publication of Chicago's most famous and accomplished Rican poet, the author of *Despertando* (1971) and *Satin City Lullaby* (1987) and leader of the city's Street Sounds jazz-poetry group--poems both old and (mainly) recent distilling preoccupations present in the author's work in the past two-plus decades. A Whitmanesque Rican whose traumatic slap by the Chicago wind opens his eyes to the forces sending Ricans and so many others to poverty, drugs, loss of security and identity itself, Hernández presents poems filled with humor, sentiment and hope. Some social protest but now also much private, sometimes amusing, musing meditation by an poet recently made aware of his own mortality.

Hernández-Cruz, Victor. *Rhythm, Content and Flavor: New and Selected Poems*. APP, 1988.
Nineteen new poems forming a chapter entitled "Islandis," plus a selection from *Snaps* (1969), *Mainland* (1973), *Tropicalization* (1976) and

By Lingual Wholes (1982). Free-form poetry and prose poems using bilingual and bicultural motives that bring together New York and other U.S. value worlds while emulating popular Caribbean musical rhythms and forms in their search for a rich poetic language based on *barrio* speech but reaching toward a more introspective orientation than many other Nuyorican writers.

Hernández Cruz, Victor. *Red Beans*. Minneapolis, MN: Coffee House Press, 1991.
Chants, prayers, celebrations and testimonies in this collection of verse and prose poems, covering the poet's years in New York, San Francisco, and Puerto Rico (*MRC*--NR).

Laviera, Tato. *La Carreta Made a U-Turn*. APP, 1984.
Reversing the negative vision of Rene Marqués's *Carreta*, Laviera's book (1979) uses New York *boricua* rhythms to transcend Nuyorican cynicism and despair, to celebrate what has been and can be preserved, transformed and gained after cultural pain and loss.

Laviera, Tato. *Enclave*. APP, 1985.
Rhythmic songs, skillful, graceful bilingualisms celebrating Rican life struggles, this 1981 prize-winner presents sharp portraits of New York's enclave dwellers.

Laviera, Tato. *AmeRícan*. APP, 1985.
Introduced by Wolfgang Binder, Laviera's third collection portrays New York ethnic diversity and examines the traditions of several cultural groups, while exploring the effort to forge a new Puerto Rican identity.

Laviera, Tato. *Mainstream Ethics*. APP, 1988.
"In the past Laviera redirected Hispanics to invest culture and emotion in the reality of the Metropolis, [but here] he affirms that Hispanic language and lore, art and history are transforming the national culture and identity of the United States. It is not the role of Hispanics to follow the dictates of a shadowy norm, an illusive *main- stream*, but to remain faithful to their collective and individual identities ... to either lay claim to mainstream territory or disprove its very existence" (APP).

Meléndez, Jesús Papoleto. *Street Poetry and Other Poems*. NY: Barlenmir, 1972.
People of the *barrio*, in a first book by a Nuyorican poet associated with Pedro Pietri and José Angel Figueroa.

Ortiz Cofer, Judith. *Terms of Survival*. APP, 1987.
"A cultural legacy and a woman's desire 'to be released from rituals'--these are the terms that Ortiz Cofer confronts in her poetic dialectic of survival. Cultural icons, customs and rites of passage take root in an imagery that is lush, tropical and piercing" (APP).

Pietri, Pedro. *Puerto Rican Obituary*. NY: Monthly Review P., 1973.
The famous title poem and others constitute one of the early classic statements of Nuyorican poetry. "Pietri uses irony, a scathing humor and the grotesque to awaken Puerto Ricans to the social realities around them (segregation, unemployment; exploitation by employers, merchants, and slumlords; drug addiction; and criminality) and to expose the falseness of the 'American Dream.' But mostly his poems address 'false consciousness,' the 'colonized' mentality of Puerto Ricans who have 'bought into' the 'system.' ... [Pietri's book] is an attempt to help Puerto Ricans 'kick' the consumerist 'habit' ... ; to help them withdraw from the false images of America and of themselves produced by the media to a space of resistance outside consumerism ... This space of resistance is identified ... with a 'true self,' a true ethnic identity, an idyllic Puerto Rico or a 'tropicalized' urban space transformed into a mythical Puerto Rico" (Arnaldo Cruz-Malavé, in *ADE*, 91: 48).

Pietri, Pedro. *Traffic Violations*. NJ: Waterfront Press, 1983.
Eighty poems, including "I Hate Trees," his acclaimed elegy. Pietri's verve and originality emerge, even as he shows more of himself and his dreams in his constant moves against the oncoming traffic. Harsh, deep laughter, tragicomedy and irony in a key Nuyorican work which shows "a disappearance of the utopic element that served as a counterpoint to [Pietri's] demythification of 'false consciousness' and ... of the didactic persona" of Pietri's earlier work (Cruz-Malavé, in *ADE*, 91: 49).

Piñero, Miguel. *La Bodega Sold Dreams*. APP, 1980.
The late writer's best work in poetry, an angry and ironic view of city

life and its marginal types, mixing ghetto slang, macho posturing, and a rough-exterior sentimental quality that disarms criticism.

*Pursifull, Carmen M. *Carmen by Moonlight.* Champaign, IL: Self-published, 1982.
A first volume by a veteran of the New York Puerto Rican scene of the 1950s, focusing on some of her past experiences as mambo dancer, wife, and mother, as well as her recent life as middle-age midwest transplant. Erotic, uneven, sometimes funny or mystical, this book shows a poet struggling to be born.

*Pursifull, Carmen M. *The Twenty-four Hour Wake.* Urbana, IL: The Red Herring Press, 1989.
A series of poems tracing the hours of the day seen as life phases and dealing with such themes as time, space and energy, desire, hope, resignation and death, showing the influence of quantum theory and mysticism on a woman whose Nuyorican roots and rhythms are here overlaid (if not overwhelmed) by Midwest Anglo life.

*Pursifull, Carmen M. *Manhattan Memories.* Barstow, CA: Esoterica Press, 1989.
A Puerto Rican woman's *Mambo Kings* as verse in a book where the poems tell a story and where the final text in fact becomes a narrative without stanzas. Pursifull now focuses on one dimension of her first book--her life as niteclub dancer and partner of Killer Joe Piro during the Latin music craze of the 1950s.

*Pursifull, Carmen. *Elsewhere in a Parallel Universe.* Intro. Dimitri Mihalas. Urbana, IL: The Red Herring Press, 1992.
A book of memories and meditations, imaginings and speculations, quantum physics and mystic revelations. Subliminal communications with a "parallel universe," calls, responses--with much family and personal musing, some politics and a few, though very few, Latino references (cf. "Elsewhere/ Wave #3). How have Manhattan memories led to this? The introduction by a U. of Illinois Astronomy professor urges we see the poems in function of relativity, indeterminacy and those dimensions of modern physics from which we may generalize about our unfixed, undulating world.

Umpierre, Luz María. *Y otras desgracias.* Bloomington: Third Woman Press, 1985.
Unconventional, often aggressive and biting poems by a university professor who picks up on the title of a prior work by José Luis González and offers a feminist lesbian perspective in this bilingual collection.

2. U.S. Puerto Rican Personal Narrative and Novel

Barreto, Lefty (Manuel). *Nobody's Hero.* NY: New American Library, 1977.
An autobiographical novel about coming of age in the New York *barrio*. The book presents the cultural problems of U.S. Puerto Ricans, as they attempt to hold on to their language and values. But in the main the work centers on housing, employment and family problems that lead to crime, runins with the law and imprisonment. Often compared to Piri Thomas's *Down These Mean Streets*, this book has been used in classes of social work education because of its emphasis on neighborhood relations with police and social service workers.

Cintrón, N. Humberto. *Frankie Christo.* NY: Taino, 1972.
As rival gangs go to war in Spanish Harlem, the protagonist comes to see the destructiveness of *barrio* life and decides to "better himself" through education.

Cruz, Nicky and Buckingham, Jamie. *Run, Baby, Run.* Plainfield, NJ: Logos, 1968.
From gang member to evangelist preacher: an autobiography designed to woo the reader to Cruz's religious obsessions.

Fernández, Carole. *Sleep of the Innocents.* APP, 1991.
A first novel depicting the disruption of rural family traditions caused by Puerto Rican internal divisions and U.S. influence. NR.

Labarthe, Pedro Juan. *The Son of Two Nations: The Private Life of a Columbia Student.* NY: Carranza, 1931.
A third person autobiographical story of a young man who leaves Puerto Rico to study in New York, and who stays on to win success and good fortune. Along with the work of Juan B. Huyke, this text

represents an early pre-Depression petit bourgeois conformist and naively optimistic phase of New York-based Puerto Rican writing.

Levine, Barry B., ed. *Benny López: A Picaresque Tale of Emigration and Return*. NY: Basic Books, 1980.
A fascinating narrative emerges in this Oscar Lewis-like presentation of a Puerto Rican's immigrant experiences and his return to the island.

Manrique, Manuel. *Island in Harlem*. NY: Day, 1966.
A black and a light Puerto Rican fight over the same woman, in a stilted novel about class and race in Spanish Harlem.

Mohr, Nicholasa. *Nilda*. APP, 1986.
The first novel by the most prolific Nuyorican woman fiction writer, *Nilda* is the story of a young Puerto Rican girl growing up in the city and *barrio* in the early 1940s. Including some well-etched vignettes, this volume shows the signs of labored style and technique--but it also shows the story-telling drive that would lead to several books.

Monteflores, Carmen de. *Singing Softly/Cantando bajito*. San Francisco: Spinsters/Aunt Lute Book Company, 1989.
Pilar's scandalous love affair in Puerto Rico as reconstructed by her granddaughter Meli, who must return to Puerto Rico to re-establish her familial identity and overcome colonial and patriarchal wounds--in this first novel by a San Francisco-based psychotherapist and poet.

Ortiz Cofer, Judith. *Line of the Sun*. Athens, GA: U. of Georgia Press, 1989.
Praised by Roberto Márquez (who should know) for opening new locales and class relations with respect to U.S. Puerto Rican experience, this first novel is a "national allegory-cum-autobiography" involving the story of three generations of the Vivente family as told by a young woman, Marisol, but based also on countless stories told around the kitchen table. Perhaps more than any other Puerto Rican narrative to date, this one portrays the back and forth flow of people, family relations and identifications between Puerto Rico and the U.S., and the power of island matriarchy. It opens with a fine portrayal of the mythic town of Salud in a series of chapters that mix ethnography and magical realism, and mainly tell the story of Marisol's uncle Guzmán, who falls

for a spiritist, and eventually flees to New York. In the second part, Marisol tells of her childhood in Paterson, New Jersey, as she is torn between her assimilationist father and island-oriented mother, and only finds her own hybrid identity as woman and writer at least partially through the mediation of Gúzman. This story, told remarkably in function of Marisol's identification with the island, spiritist culture pervading "El Building" where she lives, culminates in the portrayal of a perhaps overly symbolic if richly described conflagration which destroys the project. Though marred by contrived and clumsy plotting, and story transitions, the novel contains passages of lyricism and power, telling descriptions of Puerto Rican folk culture, and rich characterizations. Perhaps the most complex of the few novels we have to date by U.S. Puerto Rican women writers, now in paperback.

Pietri, Pedro. *Lost in the Museum of Natural History/ Perdido en el Museo de Historia Natural.* Río Piedras: Huracán, 1981.
The author's first published story in a bilingual edition, showing his narrative force as he continues to expose the false illusions inherent in Puerto Rican acceptance of U.S. consumer values.

Rivera, Edward. *Family Installments: Memories of Growing Up Hispanic.* Hammondsworth, Middlesex; NY: Penguin Books, 1983.
A young Nuyorican reconstructs his family's island roots, their move to the U.S. and then his own life experiences growing up and oscillating between Puerto Rican and emergent Anglo identifications. Written in fine style and moving beyond the raw realism of Piri Thomas and disciples, Rivera tells a moving story especially notable for a carefully drawn father/son relation, the situation of generational sacrifice and the *maromas* required to survive in the tragic "New York experiment." Growing up between mafia kids and Irish nuns and priests, our young hero pees at his graduation ceremony, and is forced to wallow in excrement for trespassing black turf in his search for a statue of his great white father, George Washington. The father works himself to blindness, plays his alternative Puerto Rican national anthems, studies Spanish language oratory, experiments with fraudulent "real-ifs" or relief checks only to find himself humiliated and brutalized on the New York streets. The son, seeing what happens to those around him, returns finally to Puerto Rico to bury his father, explore his roots, and begin to sort out the forces that have made him who he is and will be.

Rivera, Oswaldo. *Fire and Rain.* NY: Four Windows, Eight Walls, 1990.
The Vietnam war in a first novel by a New York-based writer. NR.

Ruíz, Richard. *The Hungry American.* Bend: Maverick, 1978.
The autobiographical story of a young Puerto Rican *barrio* boy who breaks with his community to seek economic success and assimilation.

*Souchet, Clementina. *Clementina: Historia sin fin.* México: Self-published, 1986.
Republican Illinois Governor's "Hispanic Community" Representative some years ago, Souchet details her odyssey from Puerto Rico to her years in Chicago as wife and then divorcée who begins to build a career for herself as a reporter and community worker. Souchet portrays her husband's involvement in Chicago's independence movement of the 50s and her decision to save him, her son, and perhaps Harry Truman as well, by becoming an FBI informer and helping to place behind bars many of those misguided souls, including her husband, who were giving their place of birth a bad name in the land of opportunity. Floridly written and uncritical, this book nevertheless, with its many letters, documents, photos, etc., provides some major glimpses at Chicago's Puerto Rican world, mainly in the first Mayor Daley's heyday. Clementina is a woman formed by her class and time, hobnobbing with Anglo dignitaries, machine politicians, rising Latino professionals, and visiting Latin American celebrities; she is a Lazarillo de Tormes, a self-righteous Moll Flanders, Boricua-style.

Thomas, Piri. *Down These Mean Streets.* NY: Knopf, 1978.
The first major Nuyorican prose work, the classic of all Puerto Rican stories about growing up in New York, this is Thomas's memoir about life in Spanish Harlem in the depression and after--his identity crises, his cultural and ethnic problems, his initiation to gangs, drugs, sex and violence. From his perspective as an ex-con turned juvenile counselor, Thomas tells of initial disorientation and deviance followed by prison and reintegration into the community. Darkskinned, he has to deal with his father's rejection, and come to understand his own self-rejection. As a privileged observer of self-defeating and contradictory racist and machistic attitudes within his own community, Thomas perhaps disappoints by his position in favor of rehabilitation and "adjustment."

Thomas, Piri. *Savior, Savior Hold My Hand*. NY: Doubleday, 1972.
The sequel to *Down These Mean Streets*, this book tells of Thomas's efforts at social and personal reintegration after being released on parole. Resolved not to return to criminal activity, he must now find other ways to deal with the tensions that continue to plague his life, seeking solutions in his marriage, charismatic religion and youth counseling. Thomas attacks the parole system and underlines the need to fund innovative community work.

Thomas, Piri. *Seven Long Times*. NY: Mentor, 1975.
Here Thomas continues his self-documentation by detailing his seven years in Comstock Prison. Published in the wake of Attica and often compared with examples of prison literature like *Soul on Ice*, the book nevertheless accepts the conventional norms of penal rehabilitation.

Torres, Edwin. *Carlito's Way*. NY: Saturday Review Press and Dutton, 1975; Dial Press, 1976.
A Puerto Rican criminal, and his underworld life: the first of Torres's novels, which have been criticized as exploiting Puerto Rican stereotypes but praised for their rich portrayal of Nuyorican culture and life, for their thriller-style plotting, their inventive detailing and their skillful use of popular traditions and newly emerging slang. A judge in the New York County Criminal Court, Torres portrays Puerto Ricans profiting on the informal economy in marginal, illegal and directly criminal activity. The same hustling criminal hero appears in *After Hours* (NY: Dial, 1976), now confused by his years in prison; in a third novel, *Q and A* (NY: Dial, 1977), the hero becomes part-owner of a *salsa* club and takes us through the New York Caribbean jazz world.

Vega, Bernardo. *Memórias de Bernardo Vega*. Río Piedras: Huracán, 1977. Andreu Iglesias, César, ed. *The Memoirs of Bernardo Vega*. Trans. Juan Flores. NY: Monthly Review Press, 1984.
This important volume, a literary find, tells the story of Vega's life as an early twentieth century immigrant from Puerto Rico who comes to New York and makes his way as a worker and then labor leader in the years before the great Puerto Rican diaspora and the slumdwelling process that was to dominate the Nuyorican experience.

Vega, Ed. *The Comeback.* APP, 1985.
A Puerto Rican-Eskimo college ice hockey star is treated by a team of mad Freudian therapists for his extreme identity crisis. Vega's parody of the ethnic novel, a satire about revolutionary politics and racism, with undercover police, professors, shrinks and upwardly mobile athletes, is considered a gem by Arte Público director Nick Kanellos.

Vega, Ed. *Mendoza's Dreams.* APP, 1987.
Replete with zany New York characters, this is a collection of short stories loosely brought together by a *Decameron-style* "frame story." Drawing on García Márquez, Cortázar and other Latin American writers, Vega gives us a comic portrayal of all the major issues facing U.S. Puerto Ricans--independence, poverty, assimilation--as he portrays struggles against bureaucratic systems which subjugate and oppress.

3. U.S. Puerto Rican Short Fiction and Essays

Colón, Jesus. *A Puerto Rican in New York and Other Sketches.* NY: Mainstream Publishers, 1961; NY: International Publishers, 1982.
A series of short prose pieces written for the Communist Party's *Daily Worker* by a first-generation immigrant who saw duty as a tobacco worker, community and union activist and journalist. His book is a treasure house of reminiscences and reflections about the New York Puerto Rican community before the Great Diaspora, in many ways paralleling the *memórias* of Bernardo Vega and anticipating many of the problems that will come to the fore in the writing of Piri Thomas or the Nuyorican poets. Although suffering from a sometimes abstract preachiness that was part of the *Daily Worker* ethos, the work transcends its limitations through the elaboration of vignettes that constitute virtual "atoms" of ethnic conflict, with far-reaching implications for Puerto Rican/U.S. conflicts and possible resolutions that prove, as in the title of one of the more remarkable pieces, that "Little Things Are Big."

Cruz, Nicky. *The Lonely Now.* Plainfield, NJ: Logos, 1971.
Our evangelist author responds to letters from people in pain in a book that manages to tell us much about the U.S. Puerto Rican experience.

Mohr, Nicholasa. *In Nueva York*. APP, 1988.
A sequence of inter-related stories about the fragility of Puerto Rican life in a world where survival is an achievement.

Mohr, Nicholasa. *El Bronx Remembered*. APP, 1986.
The Puerto Rican community in New York's Lower East Side during the 1940s and 1950s, mainly from the perspective of children, replete with good characterizations and humor.

Mohr, Nicholasa. *Rituals of Survival: A Woman's Portfolio*. APP, 1986.
A moving group of stories dealing with the struggles of Nuyorican women, proving that no one model can provide an adequate picture of the different ways different women face difficult situations. A breakthrough work for Mohr, as she portrays iconoclastic women who defy traditions, dare to express their sexual desires, and to seek their own realm of freedom away from domestic definitions imposed by men and those women who affirm a male-centered universe.

Morales, Aurora Levins and Rosario Morales. *Getting Home Alive*. APP, 1986.
A Puerto Rican mother and her Puerto Rican/Jewish daughter team up to write a collection of poetry and prose exploring their complex cultural weave which involves geographical, political, ethnic and specifically feminist dimensions of identity.

Ortiz Cofer, Judith . *Silent Dancing: A Partial Remembrance of a Puerto Rican Childhood*. APP, 1990.
Essays interspersed with poems of personal recollection and portraits of those she knew by a young Puerto Rican writer seeking a means of communicating her bilingual/bicultural heritage. The power of story-telling, of a young girl's communion with a grandmother, problems of immigration and cultural dislocation, Puerto Rican female role-formation and other themes of interest in contemporary discourse in a book that has received positive criticism and awards.

Pietri, Pedro. *Lost in the Museum of Natural History/ Perdido en el Museo de Historia Natural*. Río Piedras: Huracán, 1981.
The author's first published story in a bilingual edition, showing his

narrative force in exposing the false illusions inherent in Puerto Rican acceptance of U.S. consumer values.

Rodríguez, Jr., Abraham. *Ashes to Ashes*. APP, 1989.
Including eight short stories equally divided between Puerto Rican and New York settings, this book is notable for its portrayal of the conflict between traditional values and technological progress on the island and the conflict between processes of creativity and those of cultural disintegration in New York. A departure from the ethnic biographies which Nick Kanellos sees as dominating much U.S. Latino and specifically Puerto Rican literature.

*Rodríguez, Leonardo. *They Have to Be Puerto Ricans*. Chicago: Puerto Rican Parade Committee, 1988.
A series of sadly sardonic vignettes depicting Chicago Puerto Ricans as hapless men and women who have lost many of their traditions and values and who live pained lives of insecurity, frustration, and sputtering outrage, for the most part unable to transcend their situations. Sometimes crude in the telling, but with many insights and the only fictional book published to date which examines Chicago Rican life.

Thomas, Piri. *Stories from El Barrio*. NY: Knopf, 1978.
Thomas's first collection of short stories returns to his childhood years of Puerto Rican Harlem Hell, but this time with a lighter, less violent tone, with more tenderness, humor and compassion.

Vega, Ed. *Casualty Reports*. APP. 1991.
Another innovative work by one of the most inventive contemporary Nuyorican writers. Some of these stories may seem too commercial, too sophisticated. Most present traditional Latino themes with distance and satire--the defense of honor, the pathos of immigration--as characters waver between death and rebirth.

4. U.S. Puerto Rican Drama

Gallardo, Edward. *Simpson Street and Other Plays*. Intro. John Antush. APP, 1989.
Working-class Nuyoricans portrayed in three full-length plays which show how urban socio-economic and political conditions affect psychology and behavior. The New York Shakespeare Festival produced the title play and toured it nationally and abroad; "Women Without Men" portrays female/male relations in the worksite and barrio.

Pietri, Pedro. *The Masses are Asses*. Maplewood: Waterfront, 1984.
A pretentious and superficial upwardly mobile couple subjected to wideranging, rueful, and politically insightful satire in this absurdist *tour de force*.

Piñero, Miguel. *Short Eyes*. APP (eighth printing), 1988.
The most famous play by a U.S. Puerto Rican, this award-winning work somewhat in the mode of Jean Genet portrays what happens when a white child molester is thrown in among prisoners whose machistic code makes them hate and ultimately kill him. Famous for its raw portrayals and for its grasp of racial/sexual dynamics which speak to the transformation of core cultural patterns in terms of lumpen ritual identification and violence.

Piñero, Miguel. *Outrageous and Other One-Act Plays*. APP, 1986.
Six plays all vying to be worthy of the volume's title, as they seek comedy, pathos and paradox in the projects, subways and subway bathrooms, sleasy bars and drug dens, that make New York what it is for Nuyoricans, including the hungry writer at work.

Piñero, Miguel. *The Sun Always Shines for the Cool*. APP, 1984.
The ex-cons are now street people doing their numbers on every one in the urban jungle of the title play.

5. Translated Island-Based Puerto Rican Literature on the U.S. Immigration Experience
(No Categorizing by Genre)

Carrero, Jaime. *Jet Neorriqueño: Neo-Rican Jet Liner*. San Germán, Puerto Rico: Universidad Interamericana, 1964.
A book of poems which anticipates the development of Nuyorican literature, by a writer who went to college in New York and has visited there many times since, and whose perspective, while still island-based, shows continuing interest in the New York *colonia* and empathy with the Nuyorican perspective (Juan Flores, in *ADE*, 91: 43).

Díaz Valcárcel, Emilio. *Schemes in the Month of March*. Trans. Nancy Sebastini. NY: Bilingual, 1979.
A fine work of Latin American literature, set in New York.

Fernández Fragoso, Victor. *Ser Islas/ Being Islands*. NY: Viaje, 1976.
In this work as in others, New York resident Fragoso, like Iván Silén, writes a Spanish language treatment of the immigration experience which is still primarily a "view for the island" even as it flirts with Nuyorican perspectives.

Laguerre, Enrique. *El Laberinto*. NY: Américas, 1959. Trans.: *The Labyrinth*. Trans. William Rose. NY: Americas, 1960.
This novel, set in a 1940s New York portrayed as a maze of prejudice and poverty, tells of "wandering Ricans" making "pan-Caribbean" identification with Dominicans plotting to overthrow the Trujillo regime.

Marqués, René. *La Carreta*. Río Piedras: Editorial Cultural, 1955. Trans.: *The Oxcart*. Trans. Charles Pildich. NY: Scribner's, 1972.
A family moves from the countryside to New York, in this classic play on immigration as total disaster and defeat, as exile from sacred land, as loss of family identity and integrity. In effect, the diaspora seen from Marqués's island perspective.

Soto, Pedro Juan. *Spiks*. México: Presentes, 1956. Trans.: *Spiks*. Trans. Victoria Ortiz. NY: Monthly Review, 1973.
Classic short Stories from New York by a gifted writer whose view remains island-bound.

Soto, Pedro Juan. *Ardiente Suelo, Fría Estación*. México: Editorial Veracruzana, 1961. Trans.: *Hot Land, Cold Season*. Trans. Helen R. Lane. NY: Dell, 1973.
The best treatment yet of Nuyorican return migration to the island.

6. Untranslated Island-Based Puerto Rican Literature on the U.S. Immigration Experience
(No Categorizing by Genre)

Carrero, Jaime. *El hombre que no sudaba*. APP, 1982.
The island-based writer with strong U.S. ties uses cross-cultural code switching as the mark of his style. Carrero was one of the first to use and develop the term Nuyorican. Author of a novel about return immigration to Puerto Rico, *Raquel tiene un mensaje* (1970), and *Los nombres* (1972), here he uses stream of consciousness and other techniques to tell about a man who resists societal restrictions.

Cotto Thorner, Guillermo. *Trópico en Manhattan*. NY: Américas, 1959.
Compared to the portrayal of the immigrant experience by other island writers, this novel provides some depth in depicting "the shock of arrival and first transitions ... [as] individual traumas and tribulations are woven into a more elaborate interpersonal and social context." The novel's Spanish "is ... interspersed with bilingual neologisms--what Cotto-Thorner calls 'neorkismos'" (Juan Flores, in *ADE*, 91: 45).

Díaz Varcárcel, Emilio. *Harlem todos los días*. Río Piedras: Huracán, 1979.
A fine Latin American novel, although set in New York and focusing on the urban U.S. scene.

González, José Luis. *Paísa*. NY: N.P., 1950.
A rich text by a major island figure having much to say about the "U.S. experiment" in our own times.

González, José Luis. *En Nueva York y otras desgracias*. México: Siglo XXI, 1973.
Perhaps the most famous collection by this fine Puerto Rican writer who simply cannot accept what he considers to be the growing Anglo-Americanization of Puerto Rican values and norms in New York.

Méndez Ballester, Manuel. *Encrucijada*. San Juan: N.P., 1958.
Another negative image of the U.S. immigration experience.

Vivas, José Luis. *A vellón las esperanzas o Melania*. NY: Américas, 1971.
Still another negative portrayal of the immigration/settlement process.

IV. U.S. CUBAN LITERATURE

A. Anthologies of U.S. Cuban Literature

Burunat, Silvia, and Ofelia García, eds. *Veinte años de literatura cubanoamericana.* Tempe, AZ: BRP, 1988.
Twenty-nine authors who have been living in the U.S. since at least 1970, in a wide-ranging Spanish-language collection. The editors argue that enough time has gone by since the Cuban Revolution for the bases of a clearly definable U.S. Cuban literature to be established. Those bases point to two fundamental motifs used to organize materials. The first is a realistic trend portraying Cuban history and culture on the island and in the key places of exile (New York, Miami and, increasingly, other U.S. locales); the second is a more evocative, "magical" dimension drawing on Cuban mythology in the search for universals beyond the crises of exile and diaspora. Including writers like Lourdes Casal, Uva A. Clavíjo, Roberto Fernández, Ignacio R. M. Galbis, Luis F. González-Cruz, Matías Montes-Huidobro, Mireya Robles, Omar Torres, José Sánchez-Boudy and others, the volume includes sections on Cuban and Afro-Cuban dimensions, memory and long, roots and family, the U.S. and exile experience, politics and revolution (BRP).

*Cortina, Rodolfo J. *Cuban American Theater.* APP, 1990.
Recent plays by relatively unknown writers showing some of the new (including specifically U.S. Latino) directions in Cuban plays. Included are: "A Little Something to Ease the Pain" by Rene Aloma, "Su cara mitad" by Matías Montes Huidobro, "Birds without Wings" by Renaldo Ferradas, "Once upon a Dream" by Miguel González-Prado, "With All and for the Good of All" by Uva Clavijo, and the Chicago Cuban play, "Brisas de Marianao," by *Achy Obejas and *Jorge Casuso.

González-Cruz, Luis F. and Francesca M. Colechía. *Cuban Theater in the United States: A Critical Anthology.* Tempe, AZ: BRP, 1992.
The latest addition to the growing body of work on U.S. Cuban literature in English. NR.

Grupo Areíto, *Contra viento y marea.* Havana: Casa de las Américas, 1978.
A volume of essays containing the personal testimonies of young intel-

lectual U.S. Cubans ready to re-consider their relations with post 1959-Cuba and with their new U.S. home.

Hernández-Miyares, Julio, ed. *Narradores cubanos de hoy.* Miami: Editorial Universal, 1975.
Short stories representing typical characteristics of Cuban exile fiction by eleven writers of the last two generations whose formation was primarily rooted in pre-Castro island experience.

Hospital, Carolina, ed. *Cuban American Writers: Los Atrevidos.* Princeton, NJ: Ediciones Ellas/Linden Lane Press, 1988.
An almost completely English-language collection, the first of its kind, of some of the more important young U.S. Cuban writers, controversial for its U.S. orientation. Writers include: Mercedes Limón, Carlos Rubio, Jorge Guitart, Pablo Medina, Elías Miguel Muñoz, Carolina Hospital, Gustavo Pérez, etc.

B. Works by Individual U.S. Cuban Writers

1. U.S. Cuban Poetry

Armand, Octavio. *Piel menos mía (1973-74).* Los Angeles: Freedmens Organization, 1979. (Originally published as a special issue of *Escolios*).
Disrupted identifications and dislocated feelings dominate this important contribution to Cuban exile literature which leaves political obsessions to one side. Even one's own skin seems *less one's own*, and all of life, including oneself, seems alien. The treatment of exile transcends Cuban particularities to speak to more broadly Latin American and human concerns, by a writer of such additional collections of poetry as *Entre testigos (1971-1973)* (Madrid: Gráficas UREX, 1974) and *Cosas pasan* (Caracas: Monte Avila, 1975).

Casal, Lourdes. *Cuadernos de agosto.* NY: 1968.
Carefully wrought poems representing an exile poetry sympathetic to the Revolution. The poet asserts the political nature of all poetry, and the

need for social change; she refuses to privilege feminism apart from an overall political and aesthetic orientation.

Medina, Pablo. *Arching Into the Afterlife.* Intro. Gregory Orfalea. Tempe, AZ: BRP, 1991.
An unusual collection shifting from problems of exile to ones now on cultural and spiritual transformations in the U.S. turf. The poems present a journey of hope and despair from Trenton, New Jersey to a wider world which Medina sees as increasingly godless and asleep.

Muñoz, Elías Miguel. *En éstas tierras/In This Land.* Tempe, AZ: BRP, 1991.
A bilingual collection depicting "the core of a rich historical experience which very few poets have cultivated: that of the Cuban youth who emigrated with their parents in the 1960s, their initiation into the North American environment, the presence of Cuba in their literary imaginations and their attitude toward their new existential residence...' (Juan Villegas)"--BRP. NR.

Rivero, Isel. *Tundra.* NY: Las Américas, 1963.
A creative effort involving the employment of two distinct voices to portray a frozen landscape as the expression of feelings of exile, displacement, abandonment and isolation.

Sánchez-Boudy, José. *Poemas de otoño e invierno.* Barcelona: Bosch, 1967.
Poems expressing the situation of a Cuban exile unable to adjust to the cultural world and weather of Greensboro, North Carolina; poems contrasting the U.S. environment to the gregarious, volatile and vibrant life of pre-Castro Cuba.

2. U.S. Cuban Fiction

Fernández, Roberto. *La vida es un special.* APP, 1981.
Miami's Little Havana seen as a grotesque microcosm, in a first novel written with great verve and an acute sense of satire and bilingual schizophrenia.

Fernández, Roberto. *La montaña rusa*. APP, 1985.
A Spanish-language collage of multiple and contradictory images (satirical, comic, tragic) portraying Miami's Cuban community in all its hustling opportunism, obsessiveness and vulgarity. With vivid episodes and characters, mixing folkloric, popular and mass culture elements in a manner reminiscent of Cabrera Infante or Luis Rafael Sánchez.

Fernández, Roberto. *Raining Backwards*. APP, 1988.
Fernández's first novel in English is another Miami satire, filled with riotous scenes and outrageous characters: a lovesick girl who longs to be a Dolphins cheerleader, a poor Cuban who becomes Pope, a plantain-chip entrepreneur, another "over-achiever" who launches a guerrilla war to separate Florida from the U.S.

García, Cristina. *Dreaming in Cuban*. NY: Knopf, 1992.
Three generations of Cuban women on the island and in the U.S., remembering the past, expressing varied attitudes toward the Revolution and U.S. life. Rave reviews from critics. NR.

González, Celedonio. *Los primos*. Miami: Ediciones Universal, 1971.
A highly experimental treatment of Miami life in the 1960s by the writer who has been called "the chronicler of the Cuban diaspora." The book deals with three cousins and their reactions to post-Fidel Cuban society on the island and in Miami. The two cousins who leave only become disillusioned and unable to adapt to, U.S. life--and one of them, Eduardo, returns to the island. Meanwhile, Valentin, the cousin who stayed, becomes disillusioned with the Revolution and leaves--though at novel's end he also returns.

González, Celedonio. *Los cuatro embajadores*. Miami: Ediciones Universal, 1973.
González's second attempt to portray the hopes and frustrations of the Miami community after the Revolution, this is a plotless, fragmented work marked by extreme Cuban disillusionment with U.S. life.

Hijuelos, Oscar. *Our House in the Last World*. NY: Washington Square Press, 1983.
In the mode of the classic immigration novels, this text is important

because it portrays a family arriving long before the Cuban Revolution. The Santinios come to New York from Santiago, and see their dreams dashed, as the father turns to rum, the mother to nostalgia, and their son makes his way through the city streets. Written in an elegant English which nevertheless evokes Cuban cultural roots even as it portrays loss of culture, language and world.

Hijuelos, Oscar. *The Mambo Kings Play Songs of Love.* NY: Farrar, Strauss & Giroux, 1989.
Eugenio compulsively remembers, imagines and invents the lives of his father and uncle, César and Néstor, leaders of the Mambo Kings band, who had their brief heyday as mambo and cha-cha swept New York and even propelled them to Hollywood as Desi Arnaz's visiting musician cousins in an episode on the *I Love Lucy Show*. The book portrays frustrated crossover dreams, missed opportunities, the past dragging down any illusions of American Dream fulfillment, as Néstor's marriage, career and life are held captive and finally destroyed by memories of a lost love in Cuba; and as César is in turn destroyed by the loss of Néstor, his life declining from the Desi Arnaz peaks to twenty years of abortive comebacks, apartment superintending, womanizing loneliness, old age and death. Only Eugenio the writer redeems these sadsack lives in his literary transposition of music culture in a prose that uncovers the love songs all but buried in the blur of sex, drink and U.S. commodification. Of course, the book could be re-coded and critiqued as a white Cuban vision of a predominantly Afro-Cuban music world with U.S. Afro-American hard-bop relations and white Cuban cooptative efforts. So many absences and silences in the midst of the music.

Montes Huidobro, Matías. *Desterrados al fuego.* México: Fondo de Cultura Económica, 1975.
A novel about the effects of immigration, this work anticipates Octavio Armand's work by its obsession with the body as a symptom of cultural alienation. The first half details a Cuban exile's identity disintegration and his descent into strange, eccentric behavior and perceptions; the second half shows the hero's reconstruction and regeneration, as exile becomes a process of healing.

Muñoz, Elías Miguel. *Crazy Love.* APP, 1988.
An epistolary novel about a child's coming of age and disillusionment

as he and his family leave Cuba and come to the U.S. Music structures a book which draws its name from a popular song and presents a mosaic of Cuban culture in transformation.

Muñoz, Elías Miguel. *The Greatest Performance.* APP, 1992.
A novel about sexual and political rebellion, about the price of diverging from societal and subcultural group norms by one of the more prolific and talented of the younger Cuban writers. NR.

Novás Calvo, Lino. *Maneras de contar.* NY: Las Américas, 1970.
A mixture of the writer's preexile stories and texts written after his move to the U.S. in 1960. Some of the stories portray the misconduct of privileged sectors in revolutionary Cuba, while others center on refugees in New York and Miami. A recurring motif is that of an exile unable to forget the trauma suffered during the revolutionary process.

Sánchez-Boudy, José. *Lilayando pal tu.* Miami: Ediciones Universal, 1978.
A sequel to the author's *Lilayando* (1971), this Spanish-language novel about Miami exile and interaction, written in a language reflecting more island than U.S. Latino experience, is perhaps Sánchez-Boudy's most serious attempt to focus on and foreground the U.S. experience.

Suárez, Virgil. *Welcome to the Oasis And Other Stories.* APP, 1992.
The Mariel exodus fictionalized in a novela and five stories which present the confrontation of U.S. values and ways through the eyes of those recently arrived from another universe. Written in a taut, Hemingwayesque style, with sharp dialogue and vivid characterizations.

Torres, Omar. *Apenas un bolero.* APP, 1981.
An exiled Cuban writer becomes implicated in a political killing, in a novel of intrigue and self-discovery.

Torres, Omar. *Al partir.* APP, 1986.
A short novel set in New York and based on a historical anecdote from the Spanish American War. Told through diary excerpts and interviews, the book is distinguished by its portrayal of a suspenseful escape from a Spanish military jail by a genuine Cuban hero.

Torres, Omar. *Fallen Angels Sing*. APP, 1991.
The first book in English by this writer, about a young Cuban exile who recognizes that his part in a plot to assassinate Castro has made him a dupe of those supporting and opposing the Revolution and who seeks his own identity instead of a role in a political and propaganda war.

3. U.S. Cuban Drama

Acosta, Iván. *El Super*. Miami: Ediciones Universal, 1982.
A play later made into a wellknown movie, and a prize-winner in both forms, this work portrays the gradual mental breakdown of an all-too-human Cuban male losing his way in the New York cold and the poor heating system of the apartment building he is paid to maintain. A very funny, very painful portrayal of the U.S. Cuban experience in which politics takes a backseat to the experience of adjusting to an alien world. Trying to get along, lonely for his island home, his mother and a world he knew and could understand, Roberto, the sadsack Superintendent, resists learning English and submitting fully to the Anglo-system, humoring his Castro-obsessed best friend and maintaining his friendship with a Puerto Rican who gets tired of having to understand Cuba's problems and world historical importance. Meanwhile his wife tries to retain what she can of Cuban cultural norms, and his daughter would just as soon leave them behind--as the neighbors complain, the bureaucrats close in, and we wonder if Roberto can hold onto his sanity and family long enough to get to the haven he (foolishly? logically?) seeks to find in Miami.

Acosta, Iván. *Un cubiche en la luna*. APP, 1989.
Three plays involving Cuban-style humor, word-play and melancholy. In the title work, the protagonist, living in Castro's Cuba, devises a scheme that will force him to choose between national fame and escape. *No son todos los que están...* is an absurdist play about alienation and insanity; and *Recojan las serpentinas que se acabó el carnaval* is a comic farce about Latin American revolutionaries and dictators.

Fornes, María Irene. *Promenade and Other Plays*. NY: PAJ Publications. 1987.
These plays and especially the title work brought the writer to

prominence among new wave women playwrights in the early 1970s; they established her reputation as one of the foremost U.S. playwrights.

Fornes, María Irene. *Plays*. NY: PAJ Publications. 1986.
Some key plays by one of the wellknown off-off broadway writers, including two tragic ones, *The Conduct of Life* and *Sarita*, which deal respectively with love and military life in Latin America and the sadomasochistic psychology of a New York Puerto Rican woman.

Prida, Dolores, *Beautiful Señoritas and Other Plays*, ed. Judith Weiss. APP. 1991.
English-language plays by the well known Cuban American playwright. The title play is a musical about Latina repression in a world shaped by male chauvinism and Catholicism. The "other plays" include "Coser y Cantar", "Savings", "Pantallas" and "Botanica"--works about Hispanic/ Anglo incommunication, Lower East Side gentrification, etc.

V. LATINO-TENDING U.S. LATIN AMERICAN WRITING:
(A Sampler with No Categorizing by Genre)

Agosín, Marjorie. *Hogueras/Bonfires*. Trans. Naomi Lindstrom. Tempe, AZ: BRP, 1991.
"The most recent collection by the United States/Chilean writer, it confirms her reputation as one of the most liberated and sensual of feminist poets. Departing from unique interpretations of myth ('Robin Hood') or from novel recreations of classic, canonical poems as in the trans-Nerudian 'Ritual of My Breasts,' Agosin breaks new ground in her creation of an erotic *ars poetica* that is at the same time a poetic feminist manifesto" (BRP). NR.

Alegría, Fernando and Jorge Ruffinelli, ed., *Paradise Lost or Gained: The Literature of Hispanic Exile*. APP, 1992.
A fine collection of exile writing, with only slight traces of immigration problematics and ethnic minority voicings.

Alvarez, Julia. *How the García Girls Lost their Accents*. Chapel Hill, NC: Algonquin Books of Chapel Hill, 1991.
Fifteen inter-related stories portraying the Anglo-Americanization of

four Dominican girls told in chronologically reverse order in a first book of fiction by the Middlebury college English professor and poet-author of *Homecoming* (NY: Grove Press, 1984). Daughters of an upper-class, anti-Trujillo patriot forced into New York exile in the 1950s, the girls experience poverty, culture shock and discrimination and then begin their road to assimilation into U.S. individualism and resultant familial alienation. Their experiments in sex and drugs as well as other dimensions of life in the 60s are perhaps less interesting than the evocations of the island and actual settlement process, as told in the final stories. However rich and revealing, this book cannot speak to the new emergent workingclass Dominican literature which will require a separate treatment in any subsequent issue of this bibliography.

*Badikian, Beatriz. *Akewa is a Woman*. Chicago: MARCH/Abrazo Press, 1989.
The second, somewhat expanded edition of a poetry chapbook originally published in 1983 by this Argentine poet whose Greek and New World roots are inflected by U.S. Latino currents even as she responds to Anglo-American feminism and literary norms. Poems, mainly in English, expressing her sense of tentative identifications and alienations.

Griep-Ruíz, Leo. *Daily in all the Small*. Colorado: Maize Press, 1984.
Poems by a member of San Francisco's Salvadoran expatriate community gradually acculturating into the U.S. Latino scene, following in the wake of Nicaraguans Roberto Vargas and Pancho Aguilar, and anticipating a new wave of Central American-U.S. Latino writing which will undoubtedly emerge in the coming years. This particular volume includes reflections on El Salvador in the early 1980s, as well as some sad looks at the U.S.'s Reaganite realities.

Valbona, Rima de. *Mundo, Demonio, y Mujer*. APP, 1992.
Set in Houston, this novel explores gender relations among Latin and Anglo Americans, as refracted through the introspective probings of a Central American intellectual with many years of U.S. residence. NR.

VI. LATINO CHILDREN & YOUNG ADULT BOOKS
(A Sampler with No Annotations or Categorizing by Genre)

For a catalogue of children's books of traditional and contemporary writing, including works presenting minority and new immigrant cultures today, write to Children's Book Press, 1461 Ninth Ave., San Francisco, CA 94122. Also write to Children's Book Council, 568 Broadway, New York, NY 10012.

Beltrán Hernández, Irene. *Across the Great River.* APP, 1989.

Beltrán Hernández, Irene. *Drum Beat, Heart Beat.* APP, 1992.

Lomas Garza, Carmen; illus. by author. *Family Pictures = Cuadros de familia.* San Francisco: Children's Book Press, 1990.

López, Arcadio. *Barrio Teacher.* APP, 1992.

Mohr, Nicholasa. *Felita.* NY: Bantam, 1990.

Mohr, Nicholasa. *Going Home.* NY: Bantam, 1989.

Peña, Sylvia, ed.; Narciso Peña, illus. *Kikirikí: Stories and Poems in English and Spanish for Children.* Second printing, APP, 1987.

Peña Sylvia, ed.; Narciso Peña, illus. *Tun-ta-ca-tun: More Stories and Poems in English and Spanish for Children.* APP, 1986.

Soto, Gary. *A Fire in My Hands. A Book of Poems.* NY: Scholastic Inc., 1990.

Soto, Gary. *Baseball in April.* San Diego: Harcourt Brace and Jovanovich, 1990.

VII. CHICANESQUE LITERATURE (No Annotations)

Horgan, Paul. *The Common Heart.* NY: Harper, 1942.

Kahn, Gordon. *A Long Way from Home.* Tempe, AZ: BRP, 1989.

LaFarge, Oliver. *Behind the Mountains.* Boston: Houghton Mifflin, 1956.

Muro, Amado (Chester Seltzer). *The Collected Stories of Amado Muro.* Intro. William Rintoul. Austin: Thorp Springs Press, 1979.

Nelson, Eugene. *The Bracero.* Berkeley: Thorp Springs Press, 1972.

Nichols, John. *The Milagro Beanfield War.* NY: Holt, Rhinehart, 1974.

Nichols, John. *The Magic Journey.* NY: Holt, Rhinehart, 1978.

Nichols, John. *The Nirvana Blues.* NY: Holt, Rhinehart, 1981.

Sagel, Jim. *Hablando de brujas y la gente de antes: Poemas del Río Chama.* Austin: Place of Herons Press, 1981.

Sagel, Jim. *Tunomás Honey.* Ypsilanti, MI: BRP, 1983.

Sagel, Jim. *Los cumpleaños de doña Agueda.* Austin: Place of Herons Press, 1984.

Sagel, Jim. *Sabelotodo Entiendelonada and Other Stories.* Tempe, AZ: BRP, 1988.

Sagel, Jim. *On the Make Again/ Otra Vez en la Movida: New and Collected Poems by Jim Sagel.* Albuquerque, NM: West End Press, 1990.

"Santiago, Danny" (Daniel L. James). *Famous All Over Town.* NY: Simon and Shuster, 1983.

Waters, Frank. *People of the Valley.* NY: Farrar and Rhinehart, 1941; Athens, OH: Sawallow Press, 1987.

VIII. SECONDARY MATERIALS

A. Books on Latino Literature (General)

ADE Bulletin no. 91 (Winter, 1988). Special Section: Multicultural Literature: Part IV.
State of the art essays by Teresa McKenna on Chicano literature and Juan Flores, Arnaldo Cruz-Malavé, Yanis Gordils and Edna Acosta-Belén on Puerto Rican literature.

Bleznich, Donald W. *A Source Book for Hispanic Literature and Language*. Metuchen, NJ: The Scarecrow Press, 1983.
A useful resource covering a wide variety of sources.

Fabre, Genevieve, ed. *European Perspectives on Hispanic Literature of the United States*. APP, 1988.
Papers by writers Anaya, Algarín, Alurista, Cisneros, Hinojosa, Laviera, Mohr and others, as well as by such critics as Wolfgang Binder, Bruce-Novoa, and Francisco Lomelí, selected as the best and most representative from the 1986 conference on "Hispanic Cultures and Identities in the United States," held at the U. of Paris.

Fisher, Dexter, ed. *Minority Language and Literature: Retrospective and Perspective*. NY: Modern Language Association, 1977.
Essays on Black, Chicano and Puerto Rican literature from a symposium on minority literature held in 1976.

Foster, David William, ed. *Sourcebook of Hispanic Culture in the United States*. Chicago: American Library Association, 1982.
Contains useful bibliographic essays on Chicano, Puerto Rican and Cuban literatures.

Horno Delgado, Asunción, ed. *Breaking Boundaries. Latina Writing and Critical Readings*. Amherst, Mass: U. of Massachusetts Press, 1988.
A collection with fresh perspectives in many areas--e.g., a first Marxist analysis of Sandra Cisneros, by Ellen McCracken; a perhaps overly fanciful consideration of Puerto Rican feminism, etc.

Kanellos, Nicolás, ed. *Hispanic Theatre in the United States.* APP, 1984.
Studies of Chicano, Puerto Rican, Cuban and Spanish theater in the U.S. during the past century and a half, including articles by the editor, Jorge Huerta, Tomás Ybarro-Frausto, F. Arturo Rosales, Maida Espener-Watson, etc.

Kanellos, Nicolás. *A History of Hispanic Theater in the United States. Origins to 1940.* Austin: U. of Texas Press, 1990.
Hispanic theater thrived in the U.S. throughout the nineteenth century and even during the silent picture era and then on through the depression. Kanellos adds to his prior theater studies with this volume, which includes sixty photos.

Kanellos, Nicolás, ed. *Biographical Dictionary of Hispanic Literature in the United States: The Literature of Puerto Ricans, Cuban Americans and Other Hispanic Writers.* NY: Greenwood Press, 1989.
Supposedly a "companion volume" to *Chicano Literature: A Reference Guide*, ed. Martínez and Lomelí (see below), this work contains a valuable introduction plus very good synoptic essays and bibliographies covering the works of several writers by several good critics. Some of the choices of writers included and excluded seem arbitrary (Kanellos's dislike of the "immigration narratives" of Edward Rivera and Oscar Hijuelos cause him to exclude them from the writers studied--and whatever happened to María Irene Fornes and Julia Alvarez?). The refusal, on the other hand, to distinguish between U.S. Latino ethnic literature and Latin American literature written on U.S. soil (including no effort to distinguish U.S. Rican from Puerto Rican island writing) may cause some confusion.

Olivares, Julián. *U.S. Hispanic Autobiography*, APP 1988. Special issue of the Americas Review, 1988, Volume 16, nos. 3-4.
An effort to compensate for the lack of attention given to life writing and subjectivity formation among Latinos, this text presents a useful introduction and then new perspectives on some key writers and texts. The work includes Alfredo Villanueva on "Growing up Hispanic" in Richard Rodríguez and Edward Rivera; Genaro Padilla on "Contra-Patriarchal Containment in Women's Nineteenth-Century California Personal Narratives"; William Nericcio on Chicano frontier narratives;

Donald Randolph, Tino Villanueva and Anthony Quinn on the Chicano actor's autobiography.

Ruoff, Lavonne and Jerry W. Ward, Jr., eds. *Redefining American Literary History.* NY: Modern Library Association, 1990.
A collection of valuable materials on Afro-, Asian and Native American, as well as U.S. Latino literatures, including work by Edna Acosta-Belén, Juan Flores, Nicolás Kanellos, Luis Leal, José Limón, Teresa McKenna, Teresa Meléndez and Juan Bruce-Novoa.

B. Books on Chicano Literature

1. Recent Bibliographies

Eger, Ernestina N. *A Bibliography of Contemporary Chicano Literature.* Berkeley: Chicano Studies Library, 1981.
Still a useful work, but needing thorough updating, this text contains synopses of countless critical articles and thus enables the reader to grasp the range of theme and debate in discussions of Chicano literary works and issues, especially in the 1970s.

Martínez, Julio and Francisco Lomelí, eds. *Chicano Literature: A Reference Guide.* Westport, CT: Greenwood Press, 1985.
Hundreds of entries, fine bibliographies, a useful glossary and chronology. The entries, by several important critics, include full-fledged essays on many of the major writers, as well as such topics as "Chicano Poetry" (by Bruce-Novoa), "Chicano Philosophy," Chicano children's literature, etc. Also a valuable chronology and glossary of useful terms.

Trujillo, Robert G. and Andrés Rodríguez. *Literatura Chicana: Creative and Critical Writings Through 1984.* Oakland, CA: Floricanto Press, 1985.
A valuable guide, often consulted herein, with more than 750 citations of creative and critical works.

2. Criticism

Binder, Wolfgang, ed. *Partial Autobiographies: Interviews with Twenty Chicano Poets.* Erlangen, Germany: Verlag Palm and Enke Erlangen, 1985.
Replete with an introduction, a glossary and bibliographies this work includes veteran and newer Chicano poets in interviews that probe matters U.S. critics often take for granted. Thus, some obvious topics are treated, but often serious ones that have been overlooked. Interviews with *Ana Castillo and *Sandra Cisneros have a special relevance for midwestern readers.

Bruce-Novoa, Juan. *Chicano Authors: Inquiry by Interview.* Austin: U. of Texas Press, 1980.
A key source of insights into several major writers, information about their backgrounds and how they see their role. The book also contains a significant introduction with a useful if now outdated chronology of Chicano literature, plus a bibliography.

Bruce-Novoa, Juan. *Chicano Poetry: A Response to Chaos.* Austin: U. of Texas Press, 1982.
A seminal, post-structuralist study of major pioneer Chicano poems by Abelardo, Alurista, Montoya, Tino Villanueva, Zamora, etc.

Bruce-Nova. *RetroSpace: Collected Essays on Chicano Literature.* APP, 1990.
The post-structuralist critic reveals his growing range by bringing together fifteen of his more seminal theoretical essays in a portrayal of the history and theory of Chicano culture and literature. Elaborating his initial view of "Chicano literary space," in a search now for an ever broader, open-ended and non-prescriptive approach to Chicano works, Bruce-Novoa polemicizes, chides and sometimes insults key figures in the quickly developing Chicano literary scene. Starting with a friendly polemic with Felipe Ortego, he goes on to confront those nationalistic and machistic critics whose normative definitions of the literature exclude gay and "mainstreaming" writers; he also attacks the "less sophisticated" Marxist critics who, like the late Joseph Sommers, insist on a progressive, historical thrust to the work of Chicano writers and ritics. Including such articles as "Pluralism vs. Nationalism: U.S. Literature,"

"Hispanic Literatures in the United States," "México in Chicano Literature," and "Chicanos in Mexican Literature," the book also includes a polemical essay, "A Case of Identity: What's in a Name? Chicanos and Riqueños," which contains a fairly one-sided and snide comparison of the literature produced by the two groups.

Calderón, Héctor and José David Saldívar. *Criticism in the Borderlands: Studies in Chicano Literature, Culture, and Ideology*. Durham, NC: Duke U. Press, 1991.
Supported by Fredric Jameson, this excellent anthology of state-of-the-art criticism joins with the recent books by Ramón Saldívar and Bruce-Novoa to project the new levels and directions consolidated by advancing, and theoretically-informed Chicano criticism. Calderón and the Saldívar brothers lay out the new post-structuralist/ post-Marxist frames for viewing Chicano literature and narrative. But this volume has the virtue of qualifying and enriching such perspectives with the feminist critiques of Norma Alarcón, Alvina Quintana, Sonia Saldívar-Hull and other key writers. Angie Chabram provides an overview on contemporary Chicano critical approaches, many of which are illustrated by the excellent articles cited and uncited in this note. With a fine selected and annotated bibliography including many key critical essays not published in collections.

Candelaria, Cordelia. *Chicano Poetry: A Critical Introduction*. Westport, CT: Greenwood Press, 1986.
A critical and interpretative guide covering its subject from 1967, this useful work focuses on the poets Candelaria considers the best and most famous. The author outlines the critical methods, including what she considers the most pertinent bilingual and multicultural perspectives.

Chabram, Angie and Rosalinda Fregoso, eds. *Chicana/o Cultural Representations: Reframing Critical Discourses*. Special Issue of *Cultural Studies* 4, no. 3 (1990).
Exploring the history and prospects of Chicano studies, this valuable collection emphasizes the relation of cultural forms (literature, theatre, film, graphic art, ethnography and critical theory itself) to cultural and educational institutions, structures and practices. NR.

Farah, Cynthia. *Literature and Landscape: Writers of the Southwest.* El Paso: Texas Western Press, 1988.
Photos along with essays by Anaya, Denise Chávez, Hinojosa and other wellknown poets in a volume which emphasizes geography as well as ethnic considerations in the constitution of literary texts.

García, Eugene E., Francisco A. Lomelí and Isidro D. Ortiz, eds. *Chicano Studies: A Multidisciplinary Approach.* NY: Teachers College Press, 1984.
Essays on history, politics, education, literature and folklore.

González-Berry, Erlinda, ed. *Pasó por Aquí: Critical Essays on the New Mexican Literary Tradition.* Albuquerque: U. of New Mexico Press, 1989.
Sixteen essays exploring the New Mexico literary tradition from the Spanish chroniclers to the contemporary period. With a selected bibliography of New Mexican Hispanic literature.

González-T., César A., ed. *Rudolfo A. Anaya: Focus on Criticism.* La Jolla, CA: Lalo Press, 1991.
Essays by Horst Tonn, Roberto Cantú, Héctor Calderón, Enrique Lamadrid, Maria Herrera-Sobek, Bruce-Novoa, Jean Cazemajou, Luis Leal, Vernon E. Lattin, etc.--plus an autobiography, an Anaya bibliography, three appendices, and an index, in a valuable collection.

Hernández, Guillermo. *Chicano Satire. A Study in Literary Culture.* Austin: U. of Texas Press, 1991.
A fresh approach to classic works by Luis Valdez, Rolando Hinojosa and José Montoya, as well as to Chicano culture. Hernández studies changes in the image of the *pocho* and *pachuco* as a key to the shifting terrain of Chicano literature from the 60s into the 70s and beyond.

Hernández, Manuel de Jesús. *El colonialismo interno en la narrativa chicana: El barrio, el anti-barrio y el exterior.* Tempe, AZ: BRP, 1992.
Written by a fine Latin American-oriented Chicano literary critic utilizing a theoretical model rooted in Macheray's early Althusserian appropriation and Mario Barrera's barrio sociology, this work, while appearing somewhat late to achieve its fullest impact nevertheless should

provide some special insights with respect to Chicano literature in relation to international as well as U.S. urban parameters. NR.

Herrera-Sobek, María, ed. *Beyond Stereotypes: The Critical Analysis of Chicana Literature.* Binghamton, NY: BRP, 1985.
Articles on Chicana writers, Chicanas in literature and feminist humor, including studies of Gina Valdés, Sylvia Lizárraga, Estela Portillo Trambley and Alma Villanueva by such critics as Rosaura Sánchez, Marta Sánchez, Elihú Hernández, Tey Diana Rebolledo, etc.

Herrera-Sobek, María and Helena María Viramontes, ed. *Chicana Creativity and Criticism: Charting New Frontiers in American Literature.* APP, 1988.
A collection which joins poetry and prose by many leading Chicana writers (Cervantes, Chávez, Corpi, Vigil-Piñon, Viramontes), with a group of critical essays by some of the top critics working today (Norma Alarcón, Julián Olivares, Tey Diana Rebolledo, Yvonne Yarbro-Bejarano). Based on materials presented at the U. of California, Irvine, in 1987, the book attempts to bridge creativity and criticism, U.S. and European theoretical perspectives.

Huerta, Jorge A. *Chicano Theatre: Themes and Forms.* Ypsilanti, MI: BRP, 1982.
A critical survey presenting a history of the development of Chicano theater since the 1960s. Huerta discusses the antecedents of Chicano theater, the contributions of Luis Valdez and Teatro Campesino, the emergence of Teatro de la Esperanza and other groups, in a volume which includes good notes, an exhaustive bibliography and an author/title index.

Jiménez, Francisco, ed. *The Identification and Analysis of Chicano Literature.* Binghamton, NY: BRP, 1979.
Chicano myths, folklore, language and themes as related to and distinguished from Mexican and U.S. mainstream literature in a book representing a systematic overview of Chicano literature. Questions of Chicana feminist aesthetics and bilingualism are explored in this volume, which features a bibliography of Chicano criticism and an author/title index.

Kanellos, Nicolás. *Mexican American Theater: Legacy and Reality.* Pittsburgh: Latin American Literary Review Press, 1987.
Seven articles covering two centuries of theater from the touring companies of the mid-nineteenth century up to the present. Of special interest are the studies of Los Angeles playwrighting in the 1920s, a survey of the evolution of the circus/tent show, folklore and popular culture in Chicano theater and an evaluation of Luis Valdez and other Chicano theater people.

Kanellos, Nicolás, ed. *Mexican American Theatre. Then and Now.* APP, 1983.
This collection contains interviews and studies by Jorge Huerta, Tomás Ybarra-Frausto, the editor and others, as well as plays and never-before-published vaudeville skits from the 1930s to the 1950s.

Keller, Gary D., ed. *Chicano Cinema: Research, Reviews, and Resources.* Binghamton, NY: BRP, 1985.
With contributions by Jesús Salvador Treviño, Sylvia Morales, David Maciel, Alejandro Morales, Carlos Cortés and the editor, this is the first publication of its kind, with photos, filmography and bibliographical information.

Lattin, Vernon E., ed. *Contemporary Chicano Fiction: A Critical Survey.* Binghamton, NY: BRP, 1986.
Twenty-six articles and a bibliography, in a significant collection covering many of the major figures of Chicano fiction of the 1960s and 70s, and dealing with such topics as the theory of the Chicano novel, New Mexican narratives and the Chicano urban experience.

Lattin, Vernon E., Rolando Hinojosa and Gary D. Keller, eds. *Tomás Rivera, 1935-1984, The Man and His Work.* Tempe, AZ: BRP, 1989.
A special volume in honor of the late Chicano writer and educator, this publication features works by Rivera, as well as poems in his memory, drawings, photographs and scholarly contributions. With archive inventories, bibliography, etc.

Leal, Luis. *Aztlán y México: Perfiles literarios e históricos.* Binghamton, NY: BRP, 1985.
Essays on relations between Chicano and Mexican cultures and litera-

tures, including materials on such myths as Aztlán and Anahuac, the question of the border, the possible influence of the Mexican Revolution and its literature on Chicano literature, feminine archetypes in Mexican literature and North Americans as depicted in Mexican literature.

Leal, Luis, Fernando de Necochea, Francisco Lomelí and Roberto G. Trujillo, eds. *A Decade of Chicano Literature, 1970-79: Critical Essays and Bibliography.* Santa Barbara, CA: Editorial La Causa, 1982.
Papers on all genres from a 1980 conference at the U. of California, Santa Barbara.

Lewis, Marvin. *Introduction to the Chicano Novel.* Milwaukee: U. of Wisconsin Spanish-Speaking Outreach Institute, 1982.
A brief study outlining historical and mythical dimensions (including deeply grounded and migrant patterns) in key Chicano novelists.

McCracken, Ellen and Mario T. García, eds. *Rearticulations: The Practice of Chicano Cultural Studies.* Berkeley: U. of California Press, forthcoming.
Based on a conference held in 1990, this new collection explores the possibility of the critical application of Stuart Hall's neo-Gramscian cultural studies approaches to Chicano culture and literature, in relation to related contemporary theoretical procedures. A general introduction places the conference contributions in relation to pre- and post-conference developments. A first section, "Theoretical Reconfigurations," includes essays by Elliott Butler-Evans, Carl Gutiérrez Jones, Rosaura Sánchez and Marc Zimmerman. A second section, "Gender and Chicano Cultural Studies," includes McCracken, along with Sonia Saldívar-Hull, Yvonne Yarbro, Alvina Quintana, and Norma Alarcón, on Latina writers and feminist perspectives. A third section, "Border Issues," includes works by Rosalinda Fregoso, Héctor Calderón, the Saldívar brothers, and Néstor García Canclini. The final section, "Interdisciplinary Intersections," includes anthropological, historical and other perspectives presented by George Lipsitz, Richard Chabrán, Laura Lee Cummings, Ray Rocco and co-editor García.

Mariscal, Beatriz, ed. *Mujer y literatura mexicana y chicana: Culturas en contacto.* Primer Colóquio Fronterizo, 22, 23, 24 de abril de 1987. Tijuana, Baja California, México. Colegio de la Frontera Norte, 1988.

Among the recent books dealing with comparative literary relations involving Latino/Latin American writing, this one includes several important works in Spanish on Mexicana and Chicana themes by Rosaura Sánchez, Margarita Tavera Rivera, Gloria Velázquez Treviño, etc.

Méndez, Miguel M. *La Palabra: Revista de Literatura Chicana* 3, no. 1-2 (1981): 3-120.
A special thematic journal issue centered on Méndez, including an interview with the author and essays about his work.

Olivares, Julián, ed. *International Studies in Honor of Tomás Rivera.* APP, 1986.
A rich collection on Rivera's work with recollections by Rolando Hinojosa and Américo Paredes as well as studies by many key critics.

Ortego, Phillip D. and David Conde, eds. *The Chicano Literary World 1974: Proceedings of the National Symposium on Chicano Literature and Critical Analysis. November 1974.* Las Vegas, N.M.: New Mexico Highlands U., 1975.
Pioneer essays with renewed relevance in view of Bruce-Novoa's *RetroSpace*, stressing satire, humor, national character and identity in relation to a posited "Chicano literary space."

Paredes, Américo. *With a Pistol in His Hand.* Austin: U. of Texas Press, 1958.
A pioneering, landmark study of a *corrido* involving an interpretation of border life, and questions of method related to the production, signification and reception of cultural materials. For Ramón Saldívar, the basis for understanding the emergence and subsequent development of Chicano literature; the basis also for the movie, *The Ballad of Gregorio Cortez* directed by Robert Young and scripted by Victor Villaseñor.

Ramos, Luis A. and José Armas. *Angela de Hoyos: A Critical Look.* Albuquerque: Pajarito Publications, 1979.
A key Chicana poet examined in a pioneering study with applications that are useful in approaching other writers.

Robinson, Cecil. *Mexico and the Hispanic Southwest in American Literature.* Tucson: U. of Arizona Press, 1977.
A revised version of Robinson's *With the Ears of Strangers, the Mexican in American Literature* (U. of Arizona Press, 1963), this book, while not centered on Chicano literature, is certainly valuable for comparative analyses and perspectives (see also Arthur G. Pettit, *Images of the Mexican American in Fiction and Film.* College Station: Texas A&M U. Press, 1980).

Rodríguez del Pino, Salvador. *La novela chicana escrita en español: cinco autores comprometidos.* Tempe, AZ: BRP, 1991.
A new edition of this work originally published by BRP in 1982, with chapters on Tomás Rivera, Miguel Méndez, Alejandro Morales, Aristeo Brito and Rolando Hinojosa, with key biographical, formal and ideological considerations.

Saldívar, José David. *The Dialectics of Our America: Genealogy, Cultural Critique, and Literary History.* Durham, NC: Duke U. Press, 1991.
Sophisticated socio-critiques of "New World" writing, including articles on Latin American themes (*Calibán*, García Márquez, etc.) as well as Chicano culture and literature. NR.

Saldívar, José David, ed. *The Rolando Hinojosa Reader: Essays Historical and Critical.* APP, 1985.
Essays by and about Hinojosa, plus an interview with the writer--an excellent collection on the road to a richer version of Chicano criticism.

Saldívar, Ramón. *Chicano Narrative. The Dialectics of Difference.* Madison, Wisconsin: U. of Wisconsin Press, 1990.
The definitive work on its subject, this book, primarily rooted in Fredric Jameson's *Political Unconscious* (including all of Jameson's operations with respect to contemporary critical theory [deconstructionism, postmodernism, genre theory, etc.]), and, more loosely, in Barbara Harlow's *Resistance Literature*, poses Paredes's vision of the "border corrido" as the basic "Ur-genre" of Chicano narrative, later subject to transformations in relation to changes in U.S. society and the place of Chicanos (and Chicanas) therein, leading to the novelistic and autobiographical narratives of resistance which characterized the

development of Chicano literature in the 1970s and 1980s. Studying Villarreal, Rivera, Anaya, Zeta Acosta, Arias, Hinojosa, Galarza, and Richard Rodríguez, Saldívar then turns to recent women writers, including Ríos, Cisneros, and Moraga. First he shows how, in their effort to stand against hegemonic norms, the male writers elaborated patriarchal and machistic resistance patterns found in pre-existing Chicano narrative and culture; then he points to how the women writers have been transforming and/or challenging these patterns in function of their own perspectives and concerns. At times offering more in theoretical frame than it does in concrete analysis, sometimes limited by its border-centering (Cisneros's Mango Street is described as a Chicano "barrio", when it is at most a *Latino* barrio in the making), perhaps extending and overplaying its concept of resistance, and finally too focused on U.S. canon questions at the expense of Latin American and international, as well as inter-minority perspectives, Saldívar establishes a new level for Chicano and Latino socio-critique fulfilling now the suggestions made by the late Joe Sommers and posing a frame for future developments.

Sánchez, Marta Ester. *Contemporary Chicana Poetry: A Critical Approach to an Emerging Literature*. Berkeley: U. of California Press, 1985.
A structuralist-oriented study of Alma Villanueva, Lorna Dee Cervantes, Lucha Corpi and Bernice Zamora, attempting to see the degree to which each valorizes ethnicity, gender or writerly perspectives. Sánchez seeks a model applicable to other women writers.

Sánchez, Rosaura. *Chicano Discourse: Socio-historic Perspectives*. Rowley, MA: Newberry House, 1983.
A perspective on bilingualism essential for the study of much Chicano literature, by a fine socio-linguist, critic and writer.

Sánchez, Rosaura and Rosa Martínez Cruz, eds. *Essays on La Mujer*. Los Angeles: Chicano Studies Center Publications, University of California, 1977.
An important pioneering collection of Chicana feminist writings.

Shirley, Carl R. and Paula W. Shirley. *Understanding Chicano Literature.* Columbia, SC: U. of South Carolina Press, 1988.
A survey of the key works and themes, written for the newly initiated and the non-Latino, with very good summaries, notes and bibliographies, as well as a useful chapter on "Chicanesque" literature.

Sommers, Joseph and Tomás Ybarra-Frausto. *Modern Chicano Writers: A Collection of Critical Essays.* Englewood Cliffs, NJ: Prentice-Hall, Inc., 1979.
Key essays by the editors and others, with a focus on folk bases and socio-historical perspectives, aand critical approaches to Tomás Rivera.

Tatum, Charles. *Chicano Literature.* Boston: Twayne, 1982.
A useful survey and summary of key books, themes, etc., with notes and bibliographical materials. It contains much information about literature before 1960, as well as developments up to 1980.

El Teatro Campesino: The First Twenty Years. San Juan Bautista, CA: El Teatro Campesino, 1985.
The evolution of the best known Chicano theater group through articles, photographs and notes.

Valdez, Luis. *Actos: El Teatro Campesino.* San Juan Bautista, CA: La Cucaracha Press, 1971.
Essays, including "Notes on Chicano Theatre" and "Actos," important for understanding the early work of Valdez and his theater group.

Vasallo, Paul, ed. *The Magic of Words: Rudolfo A. Anaya and His Writings.* Albuquerque: U. of New Mexico Press, 1982.
A few essays by and about Anaya, with an annotated bibliography.

C. Books on U.S. Puerto Rican Literature

Carrero, Jaime/ Robert F. Muckley. *Notes on Neorican Seminar.* San Germán: Interamerican University, 1972.
The record of an early effort to define Nuyorican identity.

Fernández Olmos, Margarite. *Sobre la literatura puertorriqueña de aquí y de allá: aproximaciones feministas.* Santo Domingo: Editora Alfa y Omega, 1989.
A study of island and New York women's writing, including the question of New York influences on Etnairis Rivera, and a comparative analysis of Nicholasa Mohr and Magali García Ramis, in a text which makes valuable contributions and points to commonalities (e.g., the attack on patriarchal norms), but tends to underplay differences and tensions.

Flores, Juan. *Divided Borders.* APP, 1992.
The outstanding sociologist of U.S. Puerto Rican culture finally brings together a collection of his essays into a volume that should provide the basis for the development of a more coherent approach to U.S. Puerto Rican literature in the years to come. Included are Flores's fine overview article with George Yúdice, "Living Borders/Buscando América: Languages of Latino Self Formation," as well as some works which set forth some of the bases for Puerto Rican literary studies: "Puerto Rican Literature in the United States: Stages and Perspectives," "Divided Arrival: Narratives of the Puerto Rican Migration," "Rappin', Writin', and Breakin'." Many other articles join to make *Divided Borders* a major statement, and an antidote to those who underplay and misconceive dimensions of U.S. Puerto Rican culture and literature.

Foster, David William, ed. *Puerto Rican Literature. A Bibliography of Secondary Sources.* Westport, CT: Greenwood, 1983.
Mainly on island materials, this text also lists Nuyorican texts.

Mohr, Eugene. *The Nuyorican Experience: Literature of the Puerto Rican Minority.* Westport, CT: Greenwood, 1982.
One of the most extensive studies of Nuyorican literature to date, including very good analyses of Jesus Colón, Bernardo Vega, Piri Thomas, Nicholasa Mohr and some of the key poets and playwrights.

Rodríguez de la Laguna, Asela, ed. *Images and Identities: The Puerto Rican in a Two World Context*. New Brunswick, NJ: Transaction Books, 1987. Trans. of *Imágenes e identidades: el puertorriqueño en la literatura*. Río Piedras: Ediciones Huruacán, 1985.
A key text for the study of U.S. Puerto Rican literature.

Turner, Faythe. *U.S. Puerto Rican Writers on the Mainland. The Neoricans*. Amherst, MA: U. of Massachusetts, 1978.
A dissertation that is one of the few book-length studies of its subject.

D. *Books on U.S. Cuban Literature*

Gutiérrez de la Solana, Alberto. *Investigación crítica literaria y lingüistica cubana*. Montclair, NJ: Senda Nueva de Ediciones, 1978.
This volume lists over 160 Cuban writers in the U.S., making no overt indications about which might be writing a U.S. ethnic literature.

Muñoz, Elías Miguel. *Desde ésta orilla: Poesía cubana en el exilio*. Madrid: Editorial Betances, 1988.
This text by the author of *Crazy Love* and *Los viajes de Cuchumbambe* (1984) explores the various dimensions, problems and attitudes pertaining to Cuban exile literature. Muñoz's work suggests that such typical themes of this literature (disorientation, nostalgia, and gradual awakening to new surroundings, etc.) common among great numbers of U.S.-based Cubans, are not so different from themes prevalent among other U.S. Latinos and provide some bases of unity.

Sánchez-Boudy, José. *Historia de la literatura cubana (en el exilio)*. Miami: Editorial Universal, 1975.
Actually dealing with the Cuban novel in exile, this volume also points to some beginning concern for U.S. Cuban contexts.

About *MARC ZIMMERMAN*

A professor in the Latin American Studies Program of the U. of Illinois at Chicago, Zimmerman earned a doctorate in Comparative Literature from the U. of California, San Diego. He has taught at San Diego State U., the U. of Michigan and McGill U.; he has also worked in the Literature Section of the Nicaragua's Ministry of Culture and in various Midwest Latino community service agencies. He has published numerous articles in the Sociology of Literature and Culture, with applications above all to Latin American, Caribbean and U.S. Latino literatures.

His books and editions-in-collaboration include: *Lucien Goldmann y el estructuralismo genético* (Mpls: Institute for the Study of Ideologies and Literature, 1985); *The Central American Trilogy* (Mpls: MEP, 1980, 1985 and 1988); *Process of Unity in Caribbean Societies: Ideologies and Literature* (Mpls: Institute for the Study of Ideologies and Literature, 1983); and (with John Beverley) *Literature and Politics in the Central American Revolutions* (Austin: U. of Texas Press, 1990). Translator of Ernesto Cardenal's *Flights of Victory* (Willimantic, CT: Curbstone Press, 1987), he is currently preparing books on Guatemalan literature and Latino literature in Illinois.

About *MARCH, INC.*

The Movimiento Artístico Chicano (MARCH) was incorporated in Illinois in 1975 as a not-for-profit cultural/arts organization. Its goal is to promote Chicano and Latino literary and visual arts expression, with an emphasis on the Midwest and Chicago. MARCH/Abrazo Press is the publishing arm of MARCH dedicated to the publication of chapbooks and perfectbound books by and about Chicanos, Latinos and Native Americans.

To order additional copies of this book or other March/Abrazo Press titles, write or call Independent Literary Publishers Association (ILPA), P.O. 816, Oak Park, IL 60303 (1-800-242-4572).

To arrange for presentations by Marc Zimmerman and the Chicagoland Latino writers noted in this book, as well as to receive MARCH publications information and purchase some of the hard-to-find books listed in this bibliography, write or call MARCH, INC, PO Box 2890, Chicago, IL 60690 (1-312-539-9638).